LIVING
KINDNESS

LIVING KINDNESS

metta practice for the whole of our lives

KEVIN GRIFFIN

SHAMBHALA

Shambhala Publications, Inc.
2129 13th Street
Boulder, Colorado 80302
www.shambhala.com

The translation of the *Karaniya Metta Sutta* is reprinted
by permission of Amaravati Publications from *Chanting Book*, vol. 1
(Hertfordshire, UK: Amaravati Publications), copyright ©2015 by
Amaravati Buddhist Monastery.

Cover art: Maslova Larisa / Shutterstock
Cover design: Stacy Wakefield
Interior design: Kate Huber-Parker

9 8 7 6 5 4 3 2 1

First Edition
Printed in the United States of America

Shambhala Publications makes every effort
to print on acid-free, recycled paper.
Shambhala Publications is distributed worldwide by
Penguin Random House, Inc., and its subsidiaries.

Library of Congress Cataloging-in-Publication Data
Names: Griffin, Kevin Edward, 1950- author.
Title: Living kindness: Metta practice for the whole of our lives /
Kevin Griffin.
Description: Boulder: Shambhala, 2022.
Identifiers: LCCN 2022011541 | ISBN 9781645471257 (trade paperback)
Subjects: LCSH: Theravāda Buddhism—Essence, genius, nature |
Kindness—Religious aspects—Buddhism. | Compassion—Religious
aspects—Buddhism. | Theravāda Buddhism—Doctrines.
Classification: LCC BQ7230 .G75 2022 |
DDC 294.3/5677—dc23/eng/20220524
LC record available at https://lccn.loc.gov/2022011541

Dedicated to the sangha of nuns and monks who have kept the Buddha's teachings alive for millennia, and especially to those monastics today who have been my guides.

In times of conflict, when the forces of hatred seem to hold sway over the world, it's easy to despair, to surrender to these forces, and to abandon the search for peace. Losing sight of all that is good and right in the world, we start to believe that human "nature" inevitably pulls us toward hatred and greed. At times like this, we must work even harder to bring peace into our own hearts, to connect with those we love, to practice tolerance of those we don't love, to face our inner demons and forgive those whose demons run wild. It is only through the determination and effort of those who have the vision of an enlightened society founded in enlightened individuals that our species will survive these times.

The brahmaviharas (divine abodes) of loving-kindness, compassion, sympathetic joy, and equanimity are the cures for our troubled world. On the personal level they heal the heart and mind, bringing contentment and joy. On the societal level they bring people together with a focus on peace, non-harming, generosity, forgiveness, and mutual care. Our collective longing for a world in peace is answered by these ancient Buddhist teachings.

Contents

Preface

This book is based on my own experience practicing, studying, and teaching Buddhism, and particularly, the teachings
on loving-kindness, or *metta*. While I'm not a Buddhist
scholar, the book sprang from my thoughts about several
early Buddhist discourses or *suttas*, and in that sense, it has a
taste of scholarship.

The teachings I draw from come out of the Theravada school
of Buddhism that traces its roots back to the historical Buddha,
making it the oldest surviving Buddhist tradition. It lives today
in Myanmar, Thailand, Sri Lanka, Laos, and Cambodia, though
it has taken a strong foothold in the West as well, often in the
form of insight meditation.

The Theravada teachings were preserved in the Pali language, an Indian dialect close to Sanskrit and one that scholars
say was very close to what the Buddha actually spoke. This vast
literature is known as the Pali Canon. Within that canon there
are collections of discourses (*suttas*) called Nikayas that I quote
and refer to:

- The Majjhima Nikaya: The Middle Length Discourses,
  considered the heart of the Pali Canon with over 150 suttas.

These were put together because they weren't long or short, but middle length. Abbreviated "MN."

- The Samyutta Nikaya: "The Connected Discourses," organized by topic. Abbreviated "SN."
- The Anguttara Nikaya: The Numerical Discourses, organized by the number of items in a list. There are eleven chapters, with the first chapter having suttas with one subject, the second with two subjects, and so on to the eleventh chapter with eleven subjects or eleven items on a list. Abbreviated "AN."
- Suttanipata: An early collection of poetic discourses that includes the *Metta Sutta*, the Buddha's words on loving-kindness and the inspiration for this book. Abbreviated "Sn." The translation I use for the *Metta Sutta* actually comes from Amaravati Monastery's *Chanting Book,* vol. 1.

In addition, I've referred to this later Buddhist text:

- The *Visuddhimagga*: *The Path of Purification,* a collection of commentaries on the Pali Canon that was put together around 500 CE in Sri Lanka by a monk named Bhadanta-cariya Buddhagosa. Some Theravadins lean more on this commentary for their understanding of the Buddha's teachings than on the suttas themselves. Abbreviated "Vsm."

Bibliographic details can be found in the References and Resources section in the back matter of this book. You'll also find a glossary of Buddhist terms in the back of the book.

LIVING
KINDNESS

Introduction

Love, love, love . . .
The Beatles

This is a book about love. Not the squishy, romantic love of films and pop songs, but something more complicated and challenging, a love without limits or conditions, a love that includes our enemies and isn't driven by our desires or preferences. This is what the Buddha called *metta* or loving-kindness.

I started writing with the germ of an idea: that Western Buddhists didn't fully understand what the Buddha was saying on the topic of metta. In the West it's mostly thought of as a meditation practice where you "radiate" kindness, and as a feeling—a feeling of warmth and goodwill—and those are certainly aspects of metta. But my study and practice and reflection pointed to other dimensions of metta, some of which weren't easy to swallow. And I thought that, if the Buddha was asking us to practice love in these more challenging ways, we ought to try.

Let me begin by telling you about how I first encountered the practice of metta.

In the fall of 1980, as a thirty-year-old musician still trying to find my place and my way in the world, I'd started practicing

Buddhist meditation. My teacher, an American monk who had recently returned from eight years in Sri Lanka, was holding a Thanksgiving retreat, five days of meditation in the high desert of Southern California at Joshua Tree. Although intimidated by the prospect of so much time in silence, with the prodding of several friends I mustered the courage to sign up, trusting that the result of the retreat would be a blissful peace and joy.

Braving the holiday traffic out of LA, we arrived in the dark, the final miles a harrowing journey down a sandy dirt track with few landmarks and bounded by treacherous dunes ready to suck our tires into inescapable desert gullies. A tiny wooden arrow reading "Vipassana" pointed us to our destination, a rambling, rustic collection of buildings sitting atop a broad, flat, and featureless mesa, a bare landscape interrupted only by the eponymous Joshua trees. We were assigned bunkhouses to sleep in and asked to skip water-wasting showers.

It turned out that the retreat was more popular than I'd expected. The small meditation hall wasn't meant to accommodate the forty or so attendees. We sat in rows facing each other, knee-to-knee and back-to-back. The only efficient way to enter or leave the hall was all together in single file. Otherwise you found yourself putting a foot between someone's crossed legs.

As with every first-time retreatant, over those five days I struggled with pain, restlessness, and frustration over the continual thoughts plaguing my mind during the long periods of silent meditation. Songs played on repeat in my head, then entire albums. I started to obsess about the possibility of an earthquake. Was this building retrofitted? Probably not. The cinder blocks would just collapse in on us. I thought about my parents on the East Coast. What if one of them got sick and they couldn't contact me? What if they died? What if I died? Who would tell them?

What were we having for lunch? And why was the person across from me breathing so loudly?

My mind was desperate for distraction, for drama, for entertainment.

The few moments of peace came when doing slow-walking meditation outside the hall or mindfully chewing on rice and veggies. My greatest moment of joy was peeling an orange such that the skin came off looking like the petals of a flower.

On the last afternoon of the retreat, the teacher led us in a loving-kindness and compassion practice. He told us to send caring words first to ourselves, then to loved ones, neutral people, difficult people, and finally all beings. By the end I felt as if I were floating above the earth radiating love to all the suffering beings around the planet.

After ringing a bell, he asked us to turn and face another person in the hall. I cringed. I hadn't signed up for this. While being silent had been challenging, the idea of interacting—especially if it was going to be about sharing my feelings with a stranger—seemed even more intimidating. But here I was trapped in the hall. I couldn't get up without causing a stir, so I reluctantly turned around to the slender, blonde woman sitting behind me. I had never met her and didn't know her name.

For this exercise, one person closed their eyes while the other looked carefully and mindfully at their face, reflecting on the suffering that this person had experienced in life. After a couple of minutes, we reversed roles. Finally, we were both asked to open our eyes and stare at each other, again reflecting on compassion and interconnection, how each of us has joys and pains in life, that despite our feelings of separation, we are actually all the same in fundamental ways.

Sitting and gazing into the eyes of this unknown woman—who

would become a lifelong friend—I felt the stirrings of something both familiar and alien, a vulnerability and openness that I'd perhaps only touched in childhood. It left me unsettled, and yet, inspired.

This was my first exposure to the power of metta. It broke through my armored heart and opened a deep well of emotion. In fact, far from an afterglow of peace and joy, the first week back home was filled with tears and confusion. Now I see that, while I had thought the retreat would clarify and resolve issues in my life, it actually was just the beginning of what was to become a lifelong journey.

Those days of retreat and its aftermath encapsulated many of the challenges and rewards of the Buddhist path and the path of loving-kindness: the fear and trepidation of beginning; the physical struggle of sitting in meditation; the mental struggle of sitting in meditation; the bliss of innocence; the longing for love; the irritation and annoyance; the confusion and despair; the insight into universal suffering; and the fearless opening to it all as it arises and passes and arises again.

This kind of psycho-spiritual upheaval is not uncommon as one opens to metta, but I didn't understand that, and instead felt adrift with the barrage of feelings sweeping through me.

I'd been taught that metta is unconditional love, shared with all beings. Along with *karuna*, compassion, it is the wish for all beings to be free from suffering, to find a path of freedom, to live in harmony and peace. It is the highest human emotion. And, I was discovering, perhaps the most frightening.

Over the succeeding years, I would continue to encounter metta at the end of retreats and classes as a kind of cherry-on-top practice that had everyone walking away happy—or at least, very opened up. Still, my teachers continued to emphasize mindfulness, insight, and concentration in the practices they offered.

That all began to change in 1995 with the publication of Sharon Salzberg's *Lovingkindness: The Revolutionary Art of Happiness*. After that book became popular, we started to see entire retreats devoted to metta practice. For many people, this was a welcome shift away from what some called the "dry" practice of insight meditation. Now talk of "opening the heart" became more central to the insight-meditation community.

The practice Sharon described, like the one I experienced on my first retreat, followed a fairly simple formula outlined in the classic Theravada commentary, *Visuddhimagga*, or *The Path of Purification*: offering loving-kindness to oneself, to a benefactor, to loved ones, to a neutral person, to a difficult person, and finally to all beings. Over the past two decades this form has been adopted across traditions, and I have heard Buddhist teachers from both Zen and Tibetan lineages guide meditations with this exact formulation. While these teachers may have had other sources for this practice, it seems likely that they were drawing to some degree or other on Sharon's work. In fact, I think it's safe to say that since the arrival in the West of mindfulness meditation over four decades ago, no other practice has had such a profound influence on Western Buddhism as loving-kindness.

Over the years, I've given more and more thought to this practice as well as the Buddha's words on metta. I have been teaching the Dharma myself for twenty years, and sometimes have the feeling that metta has become too narrowly defined, and with that definition, too narrowly practiced.

This skepticism came into focus several years ago when I was teaching metta meditation in the traditional form to a class of college students. They were assigned to report on their meditation experience in daily journal writing. Over the course of a week or so I started to discover a pattern: they were only doing metta for their loved ones—family mostly, sometimes friends—and they were avoiding entirely the neutral and difficult people that the *Visuddhimagga* tells us to send love to.

At first it didn't occur to me what was happening, but after a while I realized they were using metta to feel good. And that wasn't my understanding of the purpose of practicing metta. I'm not implying that feeling good is bad or wrong, but it is a limited understanding of the purpose of metta.

The Buddha recognized in his own practice before enlightenment that setting pleasurable meditation states as your goal was a dead-end path. Not only were they temporary and dependent upon special conditions, but they could have the effect of diverting the practitioner from the more difficult challenge of overcoming greed, hatred, and delusion. In fact, practicing in order to get a blissful experience *is* an expression of greed (for pleasant states), hatred (for unpleasant states), and delusion (that temporary pleasant states can solve the problem of suffering).

My experience with these college students planted a seed of doubt in me. Over time this doubt grew into a serious question: How many Western practitioners of metta were using it in the same way my students did? I realized this was a risky question. I was challenging the efficacy of one of the fundamental Buddhist meditation practices. Besides that, as someone who has had his own struggles with depression and substance abuse, part of me thought, "If it makes people happy, why complain?" And, in fact, I *do* feel that meditation as a palliative is a valid use of practice.

Nonetheless, I also know that it's a limited use, that getting comfort from metta isn't sustainable. This, then, is what the Buddha called "gratification, danger, and escape." The gratification is the comfort we can derive from practice; the danger is that when it stops working we may be in a worse position than we were when we started (like someone in pain who finds temporary relief in a drug but eventually becomes addicted); and the escape is letting go of the desire to hold on to the pleasant states.

This is why I've come up with the term *living* kindness. This suggests a shift in our thinking from the idea of feeling good or being nice to people and instead addresses the whole of our lives. The Dharma is not something we just practice on a cushion or on a retreat. It's meant to be lived. The question of what this would mean sent me deeper into the Buddhist teachings.

In the same year that *Lovingkindness* was published, another equally important book was released, to perhaps a bit less fanfare: *The Middle Length Discourses of the Buddha: A New Translation of the Majjhima Nikaya*, by Bhikkhu Nanamoli, edited by Bhikkhu Bodhi, an American Buddhist monk who had trained in Sri Lanka. This was the first major Western publication of this primary Theravadin text, one of the core sutta collections from the Pali Canon. Previously these teachings were only available from obscure Sri Lankan publishers, and often in fragments or poorly translated versions. Now the Western *vipassana* community had direct access to one of the key early Buddhist sources. I ordered my copy, and opened the massive tome expectantly. And this is what I encountered in the very first sutta:

"Here, bhikkhus, an untaught ordinary person, who has no regard for noble ones and is unskilled and undisciplined in their Dhamma, who has no regard for true men and is unskilled and undisciplined in their Dhamma, perceives earth as earth."

Say what?

"Bhikkhus"? "Untaught ordinary person"? "Noble ones"? "Perceives earth as earth"? What is this statement about? And what's with the repetition? And why are they spelling "Dharma" with two *m*'s? Didn't they copyedit this thing? Here I was expecting something poetic: short aphorisms, pearls of wisdom, mystical images. Instead I felt like I was back in my Old English–literature class trying to parse out *Beowulf*. Although I could see that most of this was in English, it might as well have been in Pali.

It would take time—years—for me and many of my colleagues and friends to develop an understanding of what Bhikkhu Bodhi had edited, but as we did, it became clear that this collection, and the ones that followed, were going to be very influential in the development of Western Buddhism.

In fact, it is these texts from the Pali Canon that form the basis for much of what will follow in this book.

In particular, I want to look at these ways the Buddha talks about metta:

- **In action**, what's called *sila*. While this word is usually translated as "morality," I'm interested in more than that—I'm interested in how he talks about metta in the social realm, for people who are living, working, and interacting together in family or community or even in nation-states.
- **As "non–ill-will."** Whereas we usually talk about metta as love, much of what the Buddha talked about was the *absence* of hatred, resentment, jealousy, or any other form of ill-will toward others. This raises the question, what's the difference between non–ill-will and love?
- **As an antidote to fear.** The Buddha originally taught metta to monks who were afraid of meditating in the forest. Why?

- **As nonattachment.** Here we face a huge question: How do we love people without some form of clinging or attachment? Since the Buddha says clinging causes suffering, this is a key question.
- **In relation to mindfulness.** Mindfulness and metta are often taught as separate practices. How do they interact?
- **As an antidote to the hindrances.** These are the qualities that block our meditation practice, and the *brahmaviharas* (divine abodes) act in direct opposition to them.
- **As a concentration practice.** Many of the Burmese teachers use metta not so much to "open the heart," but to focus the mind. Why? How?
- **As a liberation practice.** Metta is a dualistic practice. How can it lead past duality to enlightenment?
- **As a practice for the earth.** Several verses in the Pali Canon point to a desire not just to radiate kindness to people, but to the earth itself. How can this apply to our contemporary environmental crisis?

One simple question informs this entire book: "What is lovingkindness?" This compound is the best translation English speakers have come up with for the Pali term *metta*. As with many other Pali words, the translation is insufficient and confusing. Two words: *loving*, which in our culture is already complicated because it's tied up with sex, so "making love" might not have anything to do with affection; and *kindness*, which seems like an odd thing to add on because shouldn't "loving" automatically be kind? The obvious reason for this addition is to make clear that it's not about sex or even just liking something, but about how we behave. While love might just be a feeling, kindness is an action.

The suttas I'll explore in this book give us more clues as to what the Buddha was talking about when he said we should offer loving-kindness to all beings. One line in particular from the *Metta Sutta* has always stood out for me: "Even as a mother protects with her life her child, her only child, so with a boundless heart should one cherish all living beings."

This verse came alive for me when, shortly after our daughter's birth, my wife and I had been invited to a small private gathering with Ajahn Jumnien, a legendary Thai Forest Dharma master. When he saw us in the back of the room holding an infant, he called us forward. He had very little English, so as he fawned over our daughter, he spoke in Thai. The translator turned to us and said, "Ajahn says 'metta is mother love.'" Everyone nodded and laughed joyfully. The words went deep into my heart, as I had been experiencing the most powerful love of my life ever since my daughter had been born. Now I could correlate that love with the teachings of the Buddha.

This is perhaps the most succinct definition of metta: mother love, the archetypal vision of affection, care, and protection. The implications of this definition are broad and deep. It doesn't require us to be mothers or fathers, but only that we want to learn to love more fully and authentically.

Metta appears in the teachings as the first of four qualities called *brahmaviharas* or "divine abodes": loving-kindness (metta), compassion (karuna), sympathetic joy (*mudita*), and equanimity (*upekkha*). At times metta is casually used as a general term to refer to all four. There aren't always clear boundaries between these different qualities; they are drawing from the same well.

Here's a brief definition of each of these:

- **Metta**: the quality of wishing happiness for others and ourselves.
- **Karuna**: the quality of caring about and responding to the suffering of others and ourselves.
- **Mudita**: the quality of appreciating and taking joy in the happiness of others and in the beauty of the world around us.
- **Upekkha**: the quality of mental balance and peace that allows us to feel each of the other three qualities without getting swept away or lost in emotions of clinging or aversion.

These four are seen as the most skillful emotions. When they are called "divine abodes," we mean that when we are feeling one of them we are uplifted, removed from the usual concerns and troubles of daily life, absorbed in the most beautiful feelings. In Buddhist cosmology, proficiency in practicing these forms of meditation is said to be the gateway to entering actual places, heavenly realms. Many Western Buddhist teachers, however, view these realms as psychological states rather than actual locations or separate worlds.

However we view them or whatever we call them, the brahmaviharas are key elements for living a life of kindness and balance in a troubled world.

one

MAY I BE HAPPY
Loving Yourself

I don't like myself any more than other people likes themselves. There's nobody in the world who knows better all my failings: my impatience and irritability; my prejudices and delusions; my moodiness and self-centeredness. And don't even get me started on my past. Suffice it to say, I lived the life of a self-indulgent musician for almost twenty years. Not a lot to be proud of there, not a lot to like about myself.

So the challenge of practicing loving-, or indeed *living*-kindness, starts with the very first step in the process: sending love to yourself. Many people find this to be an intimidating order. But I think that difficulty results from another misunderstanding of metta.

You don't earn metta by being extra good or nice. You don't get metta points for being generous or selfless. Metta isn't really a part of that karmic economy. It's more of a birthright.

Here are two reasons to give metta to yourself: it's hard to give love to others if you can't give it to yourself; and your heart longs for love.

When it comes to loving others, it makes sense that, if our feelings toward ourselves are unkind, any effort to be kind to others will be adulterated. These efforts will always be colored by some form of neediness. Either we will be trying to get validation from others or trying to compensate for our lack of self-worth by being extra "good." These external efforts will never succeed as long as our inner world feels barren.

And it's that very barren feeling that makes us think we don't deserve love. We look inside and see anxiety and sadness, worry and stress, irritation and judgment. Then we equate *feeling* bad with *being* bad. In this formulation, if we are bad, then clearly we don't deserve love.

Instead of self-judgment, metta encourages us to care for ourselves simply because we are suffering: to be kind to the sadness and worry, to be gentle with the judgment and irritation. We actually give love to those very feelings. Rather than fighting with our inner life, we open to it with acceptance and compassion.

Another way we convince ourselves that we don't deserve love is when we listen to the comparing mind or the so-called inner critic. These are the aspects of our thinking that are constantly trying to establish what status or level of success, power, or achievement we have. I recognize that this way of thinking has been with me my entire life. When I was a young musician, I questioned how good a guitarist I was. As I took up writing, I wanted to know if I was better or worse than others. Even as a meditation teacher, I sometimes wonder if people like me as much as other teachers.

It's this human need to rate ourselves, and indeed to place ourselves in a hierarchy, that is even behind sexism and racism and other forms of prejudice. If you at least belong to a higher-status group—better than someone—even if you are lacking other things (power, money, career), you can gain solace from not being on the bottom.

But no matter our status or success or level of power, the comparing mind will always tell us we should be better. Witness the struggle of the wealthy for more wealth, the struggle of the powerful for more power, and the struggle of the famous for more fame. The mind will always try to convince us that we don't deserve love, that we haven't earned it, which is why the Buddha tells us in the *Metta Sutta* to give up this enterprise altogether. Here he says we should be "contented and easily satisfied," take ourselves out of the battle and find the peace of non-striving.

There's not much in the suttas to suggest that self-hatred was a big concern to the Buddha or his followers. While his teachings on the five hindrances mention ill-will "for the internal," which could mean not liking yourself or how you are feeling, there's little emphasis on this idea, certainly nothing to compare with his repeated teachings on avoiding ill-will "for the external."

One might be angry with oneself or have aversion to a feeling, but the idea that one would become depressed or anxious just based on our feelings about ourselves doesn't get much play in the Pali Canon. It doesn't seem like too great a conjecture to say that the Buddha assumed most people love themselves or care for themselves, and so it was unnecessary to make this a point of emphasis.

And so when the Buddha introduces loving-kindness to his monks, instead of saying they should radiate kindness to themselves, as in the *Visuddhimagga* form of metta, he tells them that someone on this path should be "peaceful and calm and wise and skillful," along with a whole other series of qualities like humility, gentleness of speech, and being unburdened with duties. (I'll explore the whole list in chapter 11 on the *Metta Sutta*.) There seems to be little need to say you should love yourself.

Contemporary Asian Buddhists also seem to assume that people love themselves. Years ago when the Dalai Lama was asked about self-hatred by a Western student, it required extensive discussion with his translator to even grasp the concept. Once he figured out what the student was talking about, his only advice was something along the lines of "Don't do that!"

One passage in the Samyutta Nikaya (3.8) has been, I think, misinterpreted to suggest that the Buddha said that no one in the world deserves love more than you. While this is a lovely sentiment, the actual text says something more subtle.

It begins with a conversation between two historical figures who are recurring characters in the canon, King Pasenadi and Queen Mallika. He asks her, "Is there anyone, Mallika, dearer to you than yourself?" She replies that there isn't, and asks him the same question. He replies in the same way, that there is no one "dearer to me than myself."

It's pretty apparent that King Pasenadi is testing the queen, that he expects or hopes that she'll say, "I love you most of all." When she doesn't, he quickly covers for himself by saying, "Oh, yeah, me too."

In any case, at this point, King Pasenadi goes and tells the Buddha about this conversation, whereupon the Buddha says that if you look around, you'll find that everyone feels this way, everyone holds themselves dear. His conclusion then is that, knowing how everyone feels, you should never hurt anyone; they are all precious to themselves.

This is a somewhat convoluted way of getting to the point,

but it does make sense. It's asking people to have empathy: I know that I wouldn't want to be harmed, so I'm sure no one else wants to be harmed. Essentially it's preaching the Golden Rule.

The Buddha then adds that if you love yourself, you won't harm anyone else. This seems like a moment when the Buddha might have addressed the opposite notion, that one who does *not* love oneself *will* harm another. For those of us who have struggled with self-hatred, depression, anxiety, or despair this seems like the more vital issue. The current phrase, "Hurt people hurt people," captures this idea succinctly. But he never takes up that side of the issue.

So if the Buddha assumes we love ourselves, it's worth asking more specifically what that means. In the introduction I asked, "What is loving-kindness?" Now I want to be even more direct: What is love? What does "dear to myself" mean? If we recognize that the comparing mind will never be satisfied, will never say that we are good enough or that we deserve love, then it seems that we can never find ourselves more dear than we do other people. But I think love, at least in this context, means something simpler and more basic.

This is what I think love is: When we are hungry, we feed ourselves; when thirsty, we drink; when sick, we seek care and medicine; when tired, we rest. When we are anxious, we try to calm ourselves; when we are sad, we try to make ourselves happy. When we feel spiritually barren or lacking, we seek teachings and practices to find peace and wisdom. In all these ways, we care for ourselves, and that's what I think love is—caring. And this caring for ourselves is the most natural thing. We don't have to like ourselves or believe that we are worthy to get a glass of water or go to bed. I might think I'm a second-rate guitarist and a lousy writer, but I will still make myself lunch.

Just making lunch for yourself might not seem like a great act of love, but think about all the simple ways we don't take care of ourselves, including not eating well, not getting enough rest, working too much, and not exercising. Then there are the obvious things like abusing ourselves with alcohol and drugs (funny we call it "abusing alcohol and drugs," as if the substance were being harmed). These behaviors show a lack of care for our own well-being, so taking care of ourselves is clearly a meaningful act, an act of love.

When we determine to take better care of ourselves in these simple ways, it sets us on a path of focusing on kindness, which naturally begins to reveal the inner world of self-hate.

While taking care of ourselves externally is one form of metta, when I see thoughts of self-hatred, of shaming, or of comparing, metta practice gives me a tool for responding internally with kindness. And this is what this first stage of practice points us to. You are a human being, and as such, are subject to suffering (*dukkha* in Pali). You should be kind to a person who is suffering.

When the Buddha compares metta to a mother's protection, he's talking about the same thing. A mother cares for her children not because they've earned it—children can be a huge pain—but because they need it. And with this first stage of metta practice, we learn to care for and protect ourselves. You may have seen Buddhists wearing red or white strings around their wrists. These are traditionally given out at the end of a retreat and are called "protection strings" or cords. When one student asked his teacher what they actually protect us from, he said, "Ourselves." The cords act as reminders to be kind to ourselves, to arouse metta to heal our suffering and protect us from our own minds.

Remembering to be kind to ourselves, not getting swept away with our negative thoughts and feelings is a necessary prerequisite to applying metta. Otherwise, we go through our lives repeating the same mental, emotional, and behavioral patterns. And this remembering is a function of mindfulness—*sati* in Pali. While I'll cover this key Buddhist practice more fully in chapter 7, I want to begin addressing it now.

Two things Buddhist practice strives to change are how we *experience* the world (and ourselves) and how we *see* the world (and ourselves).

How we *experience* the world refers to our emotional response to what we perceive. What happens when I get bad news? How do I feel when I'm criticized? Flattered? When I read the newspaper? When I visit with relatives? When I go to work?

How we *see* the world refers to the way we interpret information and the things that happen to and around us. Do we see things as chaotic? Do we take things personally? Are we frightened by change? Afraid of suffering? Caught in judgments and opinions?

How does Buddhist practice change the way we experience the world?

Mindfulness, with its emphasis on just being present without trying to control things, builds our capacity to simply feel feelings without being overwhelmed. We build equanimity—non-reactivity—and inner strength.

I like to reflect on the word *irritable*, the idea that in certain moods I am "able to be irritated." In this kind of mood I am more likely to experience things as annoying; irritation is easily triggered. The training in mindfulness weakens these negative tendencies. We all know we can react very differently to the same situation depending upon mood. Sometimes we can sit in traffic patiently, and other times we're pounding on the steering wheel or shouting at the other drivers; sometimes the boss throws a pile of work at us and we feel energized, and other times we're overwhelmed; sometimes we get criticized and feel motivated to improve, and other times we want to give up.

As someone who is particularly susceptible to depression, I've thought maybe we should have a word like *depressable* to describe those times when practically anything can throw me into a dark mood. My wife gets angry with me and I start planning for my life after divorce; a job falls through and I drop into despair about my impending homelessness.

Mindfulness has a powerful healing effect on these tendencies of mind. It acts as another protection, or in Buddhist terms "refuge," from the slings and arrows of life.

This is why mindfulness is so widely recommended as a stress reducer. It doesn't change the circumstances of our lives but how we respond to those circumstances. Meditation actually works on the central nervous system to bring calm to the body and take us out of the fight-or-flight response and toward equanimity. The calm and concentration that develop through repeatedly returning to the meditation object train the mind to release stress and return to balance. This release can happen in just a moment of mindfulness in the middle of our day's activities, but it occurs most powerfully when we sit in silent meditation and put all our effort and attention into letting go and being present. In these moments the entire mind-body system resets to a healthier, default state that feels natural and easeful. When this happens on the deepest levels, as it often does on silent retreat, there is a sense that this is how you are supposed to feel, how you are supposed to experience the world. We sense that we are returning to a truer version of ourselves, freed from the agitation, distraction, and confusion of the untrained mind.

How does Buddhist practice change the way we see the world?

The first thing most people notice when they begin to meditate is how much their mind wanders. They are *seeing* something critical: that the untrained mind careens from plans to memories to resentments to fears, on and on with no seeming purpose or direction. The Buddha helps us to sort out what is happening by categorizing the nature of these seemingly random movements of mind. For instance, the Buddha has us notice what he calls the five hindrances: desire, aversion, sleepiness, restlessness, and doubt. With this view, instead of seeing random movement, we begin to understand the underlying logic of the mind, that it is driven by the desire for pleasure and avoidance of pain. Furthermore, instead of believing that these thoughts and feelings are unique to me, we begin to see them as more generally human, not personal at all. This shift in seeing is the beginning of what is called "right view," the first step in the Noble Eightfold Path: a radical transformation of our understanding of reality.

How does right view work?

When applied to the problem of self-hatred, right view reveals the absurdity, even the paradox of hating yourself. After all, who is hating whom in this formulation? Even short of that insight, just questioning whether we are so flawed as to deserve to be hated begins to chip away at the solidity of this belief. If we find ourselves able to love *others*, what makes *us* so unique to deserve special censure? In fact, we discover that self-hatred is actually another form of egotism, albeit a particularly pernicious one, "I'm so special because I'm so bad."

Finally, these two effects of mindfulness practice, how we see and how we experience the world, interact with each other, supporting each other. As we see the world differently, we are less triggered, thus experiencing it differently. When we are less triggered, we are able to see more clearly in a less reactive way, and thus change our view of what is happening. These are not separate, unrelated processes, but part of the complex interdependence of everything that happens in our lives.

We can see how these shifts must also change how we see and experience ourselves, and therefore help in our task of developing loving-kindness for ourselves. When we see our thoughts through the lens of Dharma, we don't take them personally because we know they are just playing out deeply conditioned patterns. Why hate yourself for being just another flawed human being? The Dharma says we should forgive ourselves instead. We see that our struggles deserve compassion, not judgment. If you can see the value in universal love and compassion, then how can you leave yourself out of that equation?

How we experience and see the world corresponds to two of the three aspects of the Buddha's path: samadhi and *panna*. Samadhi is mind training—meditation—and is what changes how we experience the world. Panna is wisdom, how we see and understand the world. The third aspect, sila, is morality, how we behave in the world. While most Western Buddhists emphasize samadhi and panna, the Buddha actually taught sila as the start and the foundation of the path. If we don't change our behavior, our meditation and wisdom can be empty, a gratifying philosophical framework and mental massage that have no outward impact on our own or anyone else's life. Living with sila is an act of love, a way of caring for ourselves and others. It brings us a sense of safety and frees us from the poisons of shame, regret, and guilt.

PRECIOUS HUMAN BIRTH

The starting point of all Buddhist practice is waking up to the present moment: mindfulness. Many people find that just sinking deeply into this experience evokes metta as we connect with the beauty and frailty of life in ourselves and in the world around us. In fact, mindfulness and loving-kindness can't be separated from each other.

For this practice, begin by finding a comfortable, quiet place to sit. Establish an upright posture that will allow you to stay alert even as you relax. Gently close your eyes or lower your gaze.

Take a few moments to relax your body, starting by loosening the jaw, releasing the shoulders, and softening the belly. Just feel your body sitting and notice any points of sensation in your body.

Start to feel the breath in the body in a broad way, how the chest and belly rise and fall and how the air touches the nostrils coming and going.

Recognize that this simple process that we take for granted is keeping us alive. Your body opens up to receive air; the lungs take it in and transfer oxygen into the blood; your lungs expel the elements your body can't use. Over and over, moment by moment, day by day, year by year, your body is taking care of you, keeping you alive.

See how, with no conscious effort on your part, this process goes on.

Feel how fragile your body really is, the bones and flesh, the organs and veins.

Take a moment of gratitude for your breath and your body.

We tend to think of our life as a story: the past events and dramas, the future plans and goals. Mindfulness gives us another view, that our life is just this, our senses, our feelings, our thoughts, all just happening in this moment in an ongoing flow, no form or structure, no direction, just being, just life here and now.

Can you just enjoy this life in this moment? Can you appreciate the preciousness of this amazing manifestation? In the known universe, we are the only beings capable of experiencing the world as we do. Maybe there are others out there we don't know about, but right now, we are it. Is there any reason not to feel appreciation—love, even—for this miracle of life?

→ *practice*
IN THE ARMS OF LOVE

This is a simple practice I use when I'm caught in negative thinking or feelings of distress or despair.

After settling in and connecting with the breath, begin to repeat these words to yourself: "Held in the arms of love."

Sense what it means to be held in love, the comfort and safety of being protected. Perhaps bring to mind a memory of being held as a child.

Breathe in, "Held in the arms of love." Breathe out, "Held in the arms of love."

If there is an icon of compassion that resonates for you like the bodhisattva Kwan Yin, bring them to mind.

Breathe in, "Held in the arms of love." Breathe out, "Held in the arms of love."

Let yourself feel your own vulnerability, your own frailty.

"Held in the arms of love."

Sit and take in these words and feelings until you feel an internal shift toward calm and ease.

two

LIKE MILK AND WATER
Living in Community

It's easy to lapse into generalizations about loving-kindness, about opening the heart and spreading love to everyone, but as we go deeper into our exploration of metta, we want to understand how to manifest these teachings in a meaningful way. How do we *live* the practice? Specifically, I want to explore the Buddha's teachings on living in community and the implications of what he taught. This brings us to the source, the Pali Canon, where we find the timeless words, "Thus have I heard."

So begin many of the suttas in the canon. The "I" who has "heard" is Ananda, the Buddha's cousin and attendant for the last twenty-five years of his life, and someone said to have the gift of perfect recall. Because he remembered all the teachings over those years, when the sangha gathered after the Buddha's death to organize and record the teachings, it was to Ananda that they turned to recite what would become the suttas of the Pali Canon.

What I find particularly moving about this is that we are hearing the voice of Ananda down the millennia, speaking to us and telling the stories that form the foundation of this world religion. It makes the teachings immediate and personal. Here was someone who lived with the Buddha, cared for him, listened to and questioned him. Someone who sat with the Buddha as he took his last breath.

In Majjhima Nikaya 31, *The Shorter Discourse in Gosinga*, what Ananda heard is that the Buddha went to visit three monks who, we would say, were "on retreat," that is, practicing silent meditation together for an extended period. The Buddha found them in a protected forest where he quizzed them on how they were getting along and how their practice was progressing.

The senior of these monks, Anuruddha, was another cousin of the Buddha's, and he was the one who answered the Buddha's questions. The first thing the Buddha asks is if they are getting alms food. Since the monks weren't allowed to grow their own food or keep it overnight, they were completely dependent upon laypeople to feed them. This meant that, even when on retreat in a forest, they had to be living near enough to a village of some sort that they could walk there in the morning, get food, and come back without using up too much time, since their main activity was meditating.

Why would the Pali Canon record this little detail, one that has no direct relevance to the teachings? I believe it's to show that the Buddha was concerned about his followers' welfare on every level, the physical as well as the spiritual. If love is caring, then this question reveals the love and compassion he had for his monks. First he wants to know if they are getting fed. Other questions can follow.

The alms round, too, is a vital pillar of the tradition, ever binding monastics and laypeople together. One reason for this arrangement is that it puts the two communities in regular contact, so that laypeople can get teachings, as well as the karmic benefit of practicing generosity, and the monks avoid withdrawing into a hermetic existence, detached from the realities of the world. Depending on laypeople for their food means the monks must keep their teachings practical and meaningful for a broad audience or risk going hungry. It also motivates them to behave in an upstanding manner lest they be ostracized by a lay community that expects them to be models of probity.

When Anuruddha says they are having no trouble getting alms food, the Buddha asks if the three monks are "all living in concord, with mutual appreciation, without disputing, blending like milk and water, viewing each other with kindly eyes."

As we will see, this question is not asked idly or without context. There were other communities of monks who were not "blending like milk and water."

Again Anuruddha answers in the affirmative, and again the Buddha probes more deeply, asking how they live like this—he wants details.

Anuruddha answers by saying that he thinks about how lucky he is to be practicing with the other monks. He expresses his appreciation—mudita—for his community, and in particular having fellow travelers who share his spiritual aspiration and who know how to live in harmony. Despite the fact that the monks are practicing in silence, their mutual support is vital. This is a point that's often missed in Buddhist meditation circles. We put such an emphasis on individual practice that we sometimes forget how important it is to have a community with whom to share our efforts. While it is certainly useful and important to take time for solitary practice, it's very difficult to sustain intensive or even daily practice without people who share our aspiration. The Buddha emphasizes this over and over.

He explains details of this point in Anguttara Nikaya 9.1, a sutta appropriately entitled "Enlightenment." Here he tells us, with characteristic redundancy, that all the foundational elements of enlightenment depend upon "good friends, good companions, good comrades." He says that if one has these good friends, one will keep the precepts and live virtuously; one will get to hear the Dharma; one's energy will be aroused for letting go of unwholesome qualities and cultivating wholesome ones; one will be wise and understand impermanence. We can see how this might work: if you are with ethical people, you will tend to act ethically; if you are with people whose focus is Dharma, you will tend to hear Dharma; as you hear the Dharma, you understand the work you need to do, and the positive peer pressure of the community will make it easier to let go of your negative qualities and arouse the positive; putting all this together, wisdom will naturally arise.

Now Anuruddha says that he maintains "bodily acts of loving-kindness" toward his fellow monks, "openly and privately." And he says he does the same verbally and mentally. This idea of acting kindly publicly or anonymously is an interesting one. There is a big difference between, for instance, making a public donation to a nonprofit and making an anonymous one. Clearly Anuruddha sees a value in not always letting his compatriots know that he has done them a kindness, so that he won't always get thanks or praise, but must be satisfied with his personal gratification and joy in his actions.

Anuruddha's final statement is quite telling: "I consider: 'Why should I not set aside what I wish to do and do what these venerable ones wish to do?'"

When I first read this sutta, which I had discovered by looking in the index of the Majjhima Nikaya for "loving-kindness" and finding this one under "loving-kindness in action," I was a relatively new father. It struck me that setting aside what I wished to do was a lot of what parenting was about. How often had I been interrupted or been obliged to forgo some activity because of responsibilities for my daughter? And of course, bringing a baby into our life meant my wife and I weren't going to movies or out to dinner or sleeping in but instead were devoting time, energy, and resources to this beloved little one. It's certainly easier to set aside what I wish to do for my own child than for many other people, but the principle that Anuruddha is expressing is that service and caring for others bring just as much joy—maybe even more—as always acting on our own wishes. Parenting might be our introduction to this principle, but it's certainly not the only case where it's true. Caring for an aging parent, a sick partner or friend, volunteering during a natural disaster, or stopping to help a neighbor jump-start their car—there are many situations in our lives, trivial and significant, that call for us to make sacrifices.

The timing of my daughter's birth put me in a great position to ask certain questions. My Buddhist practice had ripened to the point that the year before I was invited into a teacher-training program. That same summer I was married, so for the first time since my youth, I was living as part of a family.

Here I was being asked to take more of a leadership role in my Buddhist community, the sangha, and expected to maintain a serious meditation practice, including regular retreats and daily sitting, as well as going more deeply into the traditional teachings. At the same time I had the enormous new responsibility of fatherhood—not to mention husband-hood. I was determined to make this all work. I didn't want to create a split between my homelife and my practice, so I began to explore how I could connect the two.

Since our daughter was breastfeeding, my wife was up a couple of times every night, so I took on the role of giving her extra rest in the morning by taking the baby and the dog for a long walk after getting up. Knowing my wife was getting some sleep gave me a joyous feeling as I pushed the stroller through the neighborhood in my own foggy early morning state. Reading this sutta reinforced the positive quality of that action. In fact, at that point in my life, it was much more difficult to find time for formal practice, a concern I often hear expressed by Dharma practitioners who are busy with parenting, demanding jobs, school, or other responsibilities. Seeing the Buddha praising these simple acts of kindness helped me understand that spiritual practice wasn't just defined as time spent on a cushion, but had broader implications—and challenges.

The early years of raising a child are a time when one *must* set aside what one wishes to do if one wants to be any sort of good parent. But what about other situations? If we are always setting aside our own wishes to serve others, we fall into another kind of trap, trying to earn love through self-sacrifice. As usual, prescriptive approaches to spiritual practice are risky. What I think we need to do is examine our habitual ways of being, and then make choices from that understanding. For myself, I tend more toward selfishness than selflessness, so taking these words, to do what others wish rather than what I wish, is good advice, advice that I can afford to follow more often than not.

But I encounter others who have the opposite tendency, who more often than not put the wishes of others before their own. In this case, I often suggest being more selfish, or at least making sure that they take care of themselves as much as they take care of others.

Anuruddha's next statement is equally telling: "We are different in body, venerable sir, but one in mind." What a powerful comment on our shared humanity. It reminds me of the end of that first retreat where I stared into the eyes of another person and realized how connected we all are. Just as the Buddha says that one who loves themselves won't hurt another, seeing that we share the same human struggles, the same mind, brings forth our compassion and generosity.

The Buddha still wants to know more detail from Anuruddha. "How do you abide thus?" I like this inquiry because it's all well and good to say that you practice loving-kindness in these general ways, but it's more important to get down to specifics; it's in the gritty details of everyday life that metta becomes most challenging.

So Anuruddha describes how after their alms round whoever gets back first sets things up, the seats, water, and also the "refuse bucket." After the meal, the one who returned last cleans things up, and anyone who notices the "pots of water for drinking, washing, or the latrine" need to be filled takes care of that.

In a telling aside, we learn that the one who throws away any leftovers does so "where there is no greenery or drops it into water where this is no life." This concern for the environment is an undercurrent throughout the suttas and a theme I will address in chapter 13, "Over the Entire World: Metta for the Earth."

Essentially, what we're learning is that the monks share household duties, with each doing his part and supporting the others. There may be nothing remarkable about this, but remember what the context is: loving-kindness in action. While our Western version of loving-kindness stresses meditation, what we learn from this sutta is that the roots of metta are in how we interact with others, "blending like milk and water."

While it might be pleasant and even enlightening to meditate on loving-kindness, if we aren't able to bring this practice into action in our daily lives, how transformative is it really?

When I was describing this sutta recently, one person joked that he can be meditating and feeling peaceful and loving, then afterward open the refrigerator and yell, "Who drank my orange juice?!" And who hasn't had such conflicts with roommates or family members? Someone leaves dirty dishes in the sink or doesn't take out the garbage, and someone else gets on their case. We argue about who does more and who does less around the house. We have different standards for what "clean" means or how much clutter we are comfortable with. All these issues and many more have a lot to do with how harmonious our home lives are. It's not enough to meditate and spread loving-kindness if we can't also have loving—or at least harmonious—relationships at home.

This doesn't just apply to homelife, though. Many people live alone, but we all have to deal with people whether at work, in a spiritual community, a volunteer organization, a hobby, or somewhere else. The example of living together puts a particular clarity on the issue of how we get along with others, but the broader point is the question of how we blend like milk and water with other people. This is a central question for anyone. As social beings, humans need and depend on interaction, and yet, preferences, tendencies, and habits of behavior can easily put us into conflict. In whatever social context we are operating, we need to find ways to harmonize, or we will suffer.

It turns out that there was a greater context for the Buddha's visit and interrogation of Anuruddha. Apparently all the Buddha's followers didn't blend like milk and water. According to

Majjhima Nikaya 128, at one time some monks had a divisive conflict in what came to be known as the Quarrel at Kosambi. The details of this quarrel are found in the *Vinaya Pitaka*, the collection of monastic precepts and the stories behind them, where it says that the whole argument started over a monk leaving a bucket in the latrine (presumably an outhouse) with some unused water in it. Since the water in the latrine serves the same function as toilet paper in our bathrooms, this has hygienic implications.

Apparently there was a rule that you either emptied or filled such a bucket, but didn't leave it half full as this monk had done. This simple mistake set off a dispute that had monks taking sides, one group supporting the accused and one group behind the accuser. When the Buddha came to try to help sort things out, the monks essentially told him to butt out, and he left in disgust at their behavior. This kind of split, or schism, in the sangha is considered one of the greatest offenses a monk can be guilty of since it puts the entire tradition at risk. If everyone is fighting, how are they going to practice, much less teach and pass on the Buddha's Dharma?

This experience might explain the Buddha's careful questioning of Anuruddha as well as his praise for the three monks' behavior.

From a distance, it might be easy for us to laugh at the fact that the monks at Kosambi fell into such a dispute over a bucket of water in the bathroom. And yet, how many of us have had similar arguments with family members, roommates, or partners? Women who complain about men leaving the toilet seat up; men who complain about women's hair in the sink drain; arguments about washing the dishes or taking out the garbage; and, yes, "Who drank my orange juice?!" These are the squabbles that make for an unpleasant homelife. And if this is our homelife, how can we claim to be living with loving-kindness? And further, how can we expect our meditation practice to deepen if this kind of agitation at home is filling our minds.

I think of how I behaved in my twenties when I was usually sharing a house or apartment with friends or a girlfriend. I lacked both the housekeeping skills and generosity of heart needed to blend "like milk and water." Selfish, lazy, and often stoned, I avoided many responsibilities, including housework. Needless to say, this led to regular conflicts.

All of this is to say, again, that loving-kindness isn't just a feeling, but a way of living. How we get along with our housemates or family is just as much a part of spiritual practice as how concentrated or expansive our mind gets in meditation. To miss that point is to practice a superficial spirituality.

Nonetheless, the challenge of blending in our household is not simply one of doing the dishes and putting down the toilet seat. Conflicts with those close to us arise from several sources: intimacy can make us feel vulnerable and defensive; a behavior that you encountered once or twice might be a little irritating, but when you have to live with it day after day, it can wear you down and trigger real anger; our personal preferences are much more prevalent in our home where we might expect to have control over our environment than in public or with friends; without the constraints of a social environment, at home we might express a wider range of emotions; daily long-term contact with even a beloved person can have a numbing effect on your feelings toward them as you become so familiar with their human suffering that it subsides into a kind of background noise and ceases to evoke compassion.

Because I became aware of these blocks to expressing loving-kindness and compassion to my wife, I developed a practice that goes something like this:

May I be kind to her.
May I be aware of her suffering.
May I be open to her suffering.
May I respond to her suffering with love and compassion.

The idea was to remind myself that she struggles to find happiness just like I do; that I need to let her suffering in and stop numbing myself to it; and that I need to do my best to care for her.

The message I want to impart, then, is that if you wish to express loving-kindness you don't have to be a saint or be swept away in oceanic feelings of goodness, but start by simply trying to blend with others like milk and water, to bring the spirit of non-harming into your interactions at home, at work, and at play.

There's one other understanding about the Buddha we can infer from the Quarrel at Kosambi: he faced similar challenges to those we all do in life. If we imagine that upon his enlightenment the Buddha never had any problems or difficulties to deal with ever again, we can get the idea that spiritual awakening means living in some ideal world, transcending all life's difficulties. But what we see instead is that, after a while, he became the head of an unruly organization with all the headaches that any leader must face, including rebellious, rude, and disrespectful associates. In fact, the Buddha faced far worse in his life, up to and including attempted murder (by another cousin, Devadatta; and you think *you* have a difficult family!).

Understanding that the Buddha was subject to verbal attacks by Brahmins, contentious arguments with seekers in other traditions, and disrespectful behavior from his own monks can perhaps help us to keep perspective in our own lives. If we struggle with a difficult colleague, irritating neighbor, or judgmental relative, it's not because we aren't spiritual enough. We come to understand that our meditation practice and our spiritual path aren't meant to solve all our life's problems or create a pain-free existence. The path of Dharma, rather, gives us perspective on all of this and tools for maintaining balance in the midst of chaos. The Buddha is a great example of a human being who learned to live in the most wise, compassionate, and peaceful way possible; but, above all, he was a human being, just like us.

While I've emphasized the Buddha's teaching on living together and on sangha in this chapter, I've done that partially to balance the general impression that Dharma practice is supposed to be solitary. In making that point, I'm certainly not suggesting that solitary practice isn't important. The Buddha said over and over that meditation and the development of concentration and inner peace are greatly supported by seclusion. And while seclusion can also refer to a mental state—that is, one that isn't disturbed by distractions—physical seclusion has long been identified as a vital part of the Buddhist path. Monks often live in solitary *kutis*, small huts, so that they can take time to practice alone. The Buddha suggests that you should periodically separate yourself from society in order to go deeply into practice. Group retreat, when done in silence, creates this type of seclusion. A mature practice is one that can move gracefully from solitude to community and back again.

When I began my Buddhist practice in 1980, many practitioners seemed to be focused on retreats, with little attention to living our practice in the world, or indeed, even creating a real spiritual community. Over time a natural correction to this imbalance has occurred, and today we find many thriving sanghas that support practice both in and out of retreat and seclusion. It looks to me, though, that the mindfulness movement may have even swung this pendulum back too far, so that many secular mindfulness courses—distinct from Buddhist-based teachings—neglect entirely retreat practice and seclusion.

In my own teaching, in which many of the students are new to practice, I try to encourage everyone to find a way to take time for retreat. Silent, intensive practice allows openings and insights that are precious and rare, openings that seem to require the kind of silence, stillness, and sustained practice that only the seclusion of retreat can provide.

In the larger context of the Buddha's teaching, we can put the idea of blending like milk and water under the category of sila, the behavioral, moral, and ethical aspects of spiritual development, of the path of awakening. The Buddha said that in order to meditate successfully we need to be living a life of integrity and non-harming—sila. How could we expect to develop inner peace if our outer lives were disrupted with squabbles, selfishness, and harm? Without the foundation of sila, no authentic spiritual growth is possible. And this is what the beginning of the sutta is talking about, just in the context of a monastic lifestyle. It's not difficult, though, to see how these issues relate to our own lives, even 2,600 years later.

Sila classically refers to following the five precepts of non-harming: not to kill, not to steal, not to harm with our sexuality, not to lie or harm with speech, and not to use intoxicants. These are critical guidelines for living. But sila involves more than this and touches many aspects of our lives, especially our relationships.

In my early days of practice, I overlooked the precepts, viewing them as more remedial than the kind of advanced teachings I thought I needed. This was a mistake that held back my growth for some years.

To separate action from spirituality is a common mistake among inexperienced seekers. We like to think of our spiritual practice as transcending day-to-day concerns, and hopefully ridding us of the annoyances of work, family, bills, traffic, and all the rest of what the Buddha calls "the householder's life." But this turns out to be just avoidance, something called a "spiritual bypass," the effort to somehow skip over life's mundane challenges and have a problem-free existence—by being extra spiritual.

The fact is, the Buddha never promised this.

Sila, then, is more than following the rules and being a good girl or boy. It's about the choices we make moment by moment every day: the choice to be generous and kind; the choice to be attentive to others' needs; the choice to be of service. While selfishness and rudeness don't necessarily break precepts, they might as well, because they have the same effect—harming others. And, yes, it's true that spiritual practice can be done in a selfish way, but this is not to say that sitting in meditation or taking time to go on retreat is necessarily selfish. As with all actions, the karmic impact is determined by the intention behind it.

The larger context of "blending like milk and water" is to live with sila. My conclusion, then, is that following the precepts is an act of metta. The great modern Pali scholar Venerable Analayo draws a similar conclusion in his book *Compassion and Emptiness in Early Buddhist Meditation*: "In fact moral conduct is an expression of compassion," he says.

Whether we see following the precepts as an act of loving-kindness or one of compassion, the point is essentially the same: non-harming is itself of benefit to the world. It is "how meditation practice expresses itself outside of actual sitting," as Analayo puts it.

Morality isn't just about being "good," or not taking on "bad karma," but rather about living in the world with care for others—and ourselves. This becomes more clear when we think of the positive versions of the precepts: kindness, generosity, intimacy, honesty, and clarity. The Buddha doesn't always put things in positive terms, but we can easily see that by refraining from violence, theft, sexual harm, lies, and intoxication, we are living with metta. This expresses the Buddhist principle that the poisons of greed, hatred, and delusion are not the essence of our nature, that when they are dispelled, what's left is inherent goodness.

As an aside, I find it interesting that at the end of *The Shorter Discourse in Gosinga* the Buddha says that these three monks "are practicing for the welfare and happiness of the many, out of compassion for the world, for the good, welfare and happiness of gods and humans."

I point out this particular line because Theravada Buddhism has sometimes been accused of being a selfish path in which the practitioner is only interested in their own awakening. This closing to the sutta shows the Buddha expressing something very similar to the bodhisattva vow of the Mahayana tradition.

The Mahayana, or Northern School of Buddhism, is built on the principle that we don't seek enlightenment for our own salvation, but rather for the benefit of all, and their vow is to forestall awakening until all sentient beings are freed. While the

Theravada, or Southern School, doesn't formalize such a vow, these lines point to a similar intention. In fact, the Pali Canon makes clear that the Buddha set out to teach out of compassion, certainly not for some selfish gain. These lines show that the same intention motivated his followers.

→ *reflection*

BLENDING LIKE MILK AND WATER

To work with the teachings of *The Shorter Discourse in Gosinga* I suggest you reflect on the phrase "Why should I not set aside what I wish to do and do what these venerable ones wish to do?" Consider the impact such an attitude might have in your life. Are there relationships and situations where it would bring more harmony? And are there ways in which it would be unhelpful because of your own tendency to overdo caring for others and neglect yourself?

In this practice, we seek a middle way of caring for others and caring for ourselves.

This can start simply by committing to do one intentional act of kindness each day, just looking for opportunities. We can also notice how we are already doing acts of kindness and take some joy in that. The Buddha says we should appreciate our own kindness, take it in, and enjoy the feelings that come with it.

So, this practice isn't about being a good person, but about finding how living by the principles of the Dharma enhances our lives in very real ways. This then becomes a natural motivation for acting with kindness.

three

THE SIMILE OF THE SAW
Non–Ill-Will

While the monks at Gosinga give an example of a harmonious community, the Quarrel at Kosambi may be more emblematic of human relations, both great and small. Whether with a partner, a friend, or a neighboring country, people seem to find conflict wherever they go. Perhaps this is why the Buddha seems to talk as much about "non–ill-will" as he does about love itself. *The Simile of the Saw* (MN 21) is perhaps his strongest—and I'd say most radical—teaching on turning away from hate.

"Thus have I heard."

In this sutta a series of vignettes build to a shocking description of the level of forgiveness and loving-kindness the Buddha expects from his followers. The theme of the sutta is the challenge of maintaining non–ill-will in the face of attacks, verbal or physical. Here we see one of the rhetorical teaching strategies of the Buddha. He seems to understand that a positive declaration to love everyone can trigger grasping, so instead points us toward letting go of the obstructions to love. In this way, his rhetoric mirrors the teachings themselves: letting go is the path to freedom, so he tells us what to let go of. If instead he had set out some ideal to strive for, it would just give people something else to chase after.

And again, the implication is that our natural state when rid of these negative qualities is a positive one, that when hatred is removed, love is naturally revealed, that when greed subsides, generosity is spontaneous. This is an essential Buddhist concept, that our fundamental human nature is loving and wise. The work of Buddhist practice is to abandon the things that obscure these qualities in us.

The first story in the sutta is of a monk with the odd name of Moliya Phagguna (of course, Phagguna would probably think Kevin Griffin was an odd name—tastes change). Phagguna, it turns out, has been hanging out too much with the nuns. This is always discouraged because of the risk of the development of a sexual relationship and abandonment of the monastic life. But this isn't the main point of the sutta. Rather, the Buddha wants to talk about anger and ill-will.

It seems that if another monk insulted one of the nuns, Phagguna would get angry and "rebuke him." And the same with the nuns, if someone said something unkind about Phagguna, they'd get angry as well. When the Buddha hears about this behavior, he calls for Phagguna who admits to it all.

The Buddha tells him that no matter what anyone says about the nuns, he should think like this: "My mind will be unaffected, and I shall utter no evil words; I shall abide compassionate for his welfare, with a mind of loving-kindness, without inner hate." He then raises the stakes by saying that even if someone hits the nuns "with his hand, with a clod, with a stick or with a knife," his mind should remain unaffected. While this is only the beginning of the sutta, the Buddha has already presented a challenging teaching, one whose implications may not be acceptable to everyone who hears it.

It seems as if the Buddha is suggesting that Phagguna shouldn't protect the nuns. Is it really appropriate to stand by when someone else is being attacked? This is a question that Buddhists have long debated. However, Bhikkhu Bodhi points out that the Buddha is talking about Phagguna's *mental* reaction—being "unaffected"—not how he behaves. He shouldn't get upset or angry, but this doesn't mean he shouldn't act compassionately or wisely. When I asked Ajahn Pasanno, a revered Buddhist monk, about this passage, he said that rather than a "moral injunction," he thought we were being given a vision of how to hold such a situation in our heart/mind. It's these sorts of questions that make adhering to a 2,600-year-old tradition tricky.

A secondary theme of this story about Phagguna's relationship with the nuns (and theirs with him) is the problem of bias. Because Phagguna is enamored of these women, he will defend them no matter what. He has his position, and he's not moving from it. In fact, he's willing to fight to defend it. Whereas the Buddha's attitude is that one should be "easy to admonish," as he says later in the sutta and in other teachings, Phagguna isn't willing to consider that someone speaking ill of the nuns might have a point. The Buddha—and Buddhism as we understand it today—emphasizes the importance of acknowledging what is true, no matter what our preferences, conditioning, or biases. This insistence on the primacy of fact over belief is epitomized in the Dalai Lama's famous statement that if science proves Buddhism to be wrong, Buddhism must change. Rarely do we hear such a statement from a religious leader.

Unfortunately, the commentaries tell us that Phagguna eventually left the robes, apparently not convinced, or perhaps lacking the faith needed to remain in the monastic life.

The next passage in the sutta might explain why the Buddha is so emphatic in his treatment of Phagguna. He says that, "there was an occasion when the bhikkhus satisfied my mind"—the point being, now the bhikkhus *don't* satisfy his mind. His first simile to describe responsive monks is a classic and easily understood image of horses that jump to the commands of their owner: "I only had to arouse mindfulness in them," he says, again avoiding the obvious statement that nowadays he has uncooperative monks like Phagguna.

A second simile, of a grove of trees choked with "crooked saplings," can be read in two ways. While the Buddha says the saplings represent unwholesome states that should be abandoned, a subtext could be that these noncompliant monks should be cleared out of the sangha. While I wouldn't say the Buddha was exactly frustrated, the tone of the sutta certainly exhibits some impatience toward his followers.

The Buddha now deepens his theme with a story he tells of a maid, Kali, and her mistress, Vedehika. The mistress has a reputation for being "kind, gentle, and peaceful." But Kali has her doubts, so she sets out to test whether beneath her placid surface anger lurks. This is what the Buddha calls an "underlying tendency," a negative quality that comes out under stress or pressure. (In another sutta, MN 64, the Buddha says that an infant has underlying tendencies like lust and ill-will that will only manifest as they grow.)

Kali intentionally gets up late one day, provoking Vedehika's wrath. Now convinced that her mistress has the underlying tendency of anger, she keeps pushing her by getting up later and later. Finally Vedehika snaps, giving Kali a crack in the head with a rolling pin (at this point the sutta is starting to sound like an American sitcom). With blood running down her face, Kali runs to the neighbors shouting, "See the 'kind' lady's work!" Vedehika's reputation is ruined.

Once more, the Buddha's story brings up questions that aren't addressed in the sutta. Even Bhikkhu Bodhi, who edited these suttas, asks in his own reflections whether the provocations of Kali aren't difficult to support. Certainly Vedehika shouldn't have behaved as she did, but shouldn't something also be said about Kali? I suppose that in this tale, that's not the point.

Rather, the Buddha explains the story by saying that a bhikkhu—though it's not limited to monks—can seem to be kind and gentle until "disagreeable courses of speech touch him." He's calling us out, and I can't help but feel exposed when I read this teaching. Like most people, I think of myself as a good person, but how often have I gotten angry when meeting "disagreeable courses of speech"? I've spent years trying to dredge up and abandon the underlying tendencies of defensiveness and pride that arise when criticized. In this dry and formal language, once again the Buddha captures something basic about human nature, how superficial our kindness can be and how easily we are triggered.

And now he expands the message of the sutta. No matter how someone addresses us or treats us, not only should we "abide compassionate" and "without inner hate," but we should think like this as well:

we shall abide pervading the all-encompassing world with a mind imbued with loving-kindness, abundant, exalted, immeasurable, without hostility and without ill-will.

The challenge he puts forth is that, not only should we not hate the person who treats us poorly, but that we should love them. And further, that we should love everyone and everything in the world. This is the heart of the Buddha's message, and one that every Buddhist must confront, even as we acknowledge our own underlying tendencies of aversion.

Now the sutta approaches its climax with a bizarre series of images, each one referring back to this passage telling us that our minds must remain unaffected.

First is an image of loving-kindness as vast and unmovable as the earth. He asks the monks if a man could dig up the earth so he could make the earth "be without earth." It's a strange image, someone digging away and tossing dirt aside thinking they were getting rid of the earth. Where could that dirt possibly go? If our loving-kindness were equally pervasive, nothing could disturb it.

The Buddha uses a similar image in a teaching he gives his son, Rahula (MN 62). Here he says that although people despoil and pollute the earth that, "the earth is not horrified, humiliated, and disgusted," the earth isn't bothered. He says Rahula should meditate in a way that, "arisen agreeable and disagreeable contacts will not invade your mind and remain." Whether something pleasant or unpleasant is happening, you should be undisturbed.

The image draws on the sense of groundedness that can be achieved in meditation. One popular practice asks you to imagine you are a mountain as you sit in meditation. The Buddha draws on this idea of being deeply rooted and still, our loving-kindness as stable as the earth itself.

The next image is one of the openness and vastness of space. He asks what would happen if someone brought different dyes and tried to draw pictures on empty space. Again, this is a little hard to imagine, but it's the absurdity that the Buddha is highlighting. If my ego is spacious and empty, no insults can take hold. You can attack me all you want, but your words will only pass through, incapable of coloring my mind with negativity.

This calls to mind another sutta where the Buddha was being berated by a Brahmin (SN 7.2). This Brahmin was pacing up and down in front of the Buddha telling him everything that was wrong with his teachings. I always imagine the Buddha with a serene look on his face calmly watching this agitated man spewing venom. (Many Brahmins opposed the Buddha because his teachings challenged their beliefs and threatened their power.) When the Brahmin completes his tirade, the Buddha asks him a series of questions.

Do people come to his house as guests?

Yes.

Does he offer them food?

Yes.

If they refuse the food, who does that belong to?

The Brahmin admits that such food still belongs to him.

The Buddha then says that he doesn't accept the abuse being heaped on him. "It still belongs to you, Brahmin!"

The message is twofold: not only is the Buddha not harmed by the abuse, but the abuser *is*.

The Buddha goes on, "Not repaying an angry man with anger one wins a battle hard to win," acknowledging how difficult it is not to be reactive when being harangued. The battle is with one's own impulse to strike back. Further, he claims that this person "practices for the welfare of both—his own and the other's—when, knowing that his foe is angry, he mindfully maintains his peace." This is how we bring harmony in fraught situations, by not being reactive. By keeping ourselves calm, we help the agitated person to calm down.

At a recent class I was teaching, someone brought up how behaving calmly when someone is berating you can actually trigger more frustration on the part of the abuser. This can be perceived as smug complacency. But in the case of the Brahmin, the Buddha's response has no hint of high-handedness, and is, in fact, quite forceful. While he's not reactive or angry, we could say that he is meeting the Brahmin's level of engagement or energy at the same level. He's not remaining silent, and in fact, the sutta tells us that some of those present thought he was angry, an impression the Buddha quickly dispels.

The Buddha's reaction, in fact, inspires the Brahmin to become a follower.

We can see how the Buddha's lack of ego—like space, impossible to color—protects him and frees him from attachment or conflict.

Returning to *The Simile of the Saw*, the next image is of water, specifically the Ganges. Here the Buddha asks what would happen if someone tried to burn up the great river. As anger is often correlated with heat, this image seems particularly apt. Like the Brahmin pacing in front of the Buddha, the heat of anger swells inside us, both physically and emotionally. But if our loving-kindness is cool, flowing, and vast as the Ganges, no amount of heat will burn it away.

The next image is rather obscure because it talks about a "catskin bag" that has been made soft by rubbing it. He says that a man couldn't make a crackling or rustling sound by scratching it. This might be like trying to make music with a piece of leather, something that could only bring frustration.

In all of these cases, the Buddha says that the person who

tried these things would "reap only weariness and disappointment." If we remain resolute in our loving-kindness, people will only get frustrated if they try to provoke us.

The final image gives the sutta its name and is one of the most controversial in the Pali Canon.

Even if bandits were to sever you savagely limb by limb with a two-handled saw, he [or she] who gave rise to a mind of hate towards them would not be carrying out my teachings.

He goes on to repeat that even in those circumstances you should "abide compassionate for their welfare, with a mind of loving-kindness, without inner hate."

My first impression upon reading this sutta was, "The Buddha must be crazy!" How could anyone maintain loving-kindness under such circumstances? When I hear people talking about opening their hearts with love and compassion, I don't immediately think about opening my heart to someone who was torturing me in this way. But clearly the Buddha wasn't crazy. He meant it.

Let's reflect on this teaching in a way that might be more manageable, because I don't think many of us could go as far as the Buddha suggests. But this does remind me of my college students and their tendency to avoid sending loving-kindness to difficult people. It's easy enough to develop a feeling of love toward those we care about. Not that we don't ever have negative feelings about them, but sitting in meditation and thinking about what's really important to us in these relationships, most of us can certainly arouse loving-kindness. So that doesn't really accomplish very much in terms of spiritual growth or transformation. What happens, though, when we bring to mind someone with whom we've had conflict or someone we feel negatively toward? (I've often used political figures to test myself in this practice.) What happens to most of us is that when we first think of these people, even if our heart is open, it closes. If it's not open in the first place, then an even stronger negative feeling can come up.

If we are doing the formal loving-kindness practice, by the time we get to the difficult person, we've aroused a certain amount of openness and positive feelings. In that case, when we turn the mind toward the difficult person, we'll be aware if the heart closes. At that point, we're encouraged to continue with phrases of loving-kindness even if the feeling isn't there. The *Visuddhimagga* gives another suggestion that's helpful. It says that with *neutral* people, we should try to move our feeling to loving-kindness, but that for *difficult* people we should just try to move our feeling to neutral. This seems more realistic for most of us than the Buddha's instruction.

It wasn't until I was teaching this sutta to these same college students—at a Catholic college—that it occurred to me that there was a great example of the simile of the saw in the Christian tradition: Christ on the cross. After being tortured all night, whipped and beaten, a crown of thorns mockingly pressed into his skull, he is forced to drag a huge wooden cross through the streets of Jerusalem where he is jeered at, spat upon, and further abused. Then, instead of the typical crucifixion that involved being *tied* to a cross, just for good measure, he is nailed up. One can only imagine the physical pain and how that would affect the mind. The final insult of a spear through the side completed the absolute cruelty that certainly caused pain equivalent to having your limbs sawed off. At that point, we're told that he said of his tormentors, "Forgive them, Lord, they know not what they've done." These words express perfectly what the Buddha was teaching and, in some ways, make his teaching more accessible to me. The heroism of a martyr has some resonance that simply being sawed apart by bandits doesn't. This model of forgiveness is deeply embedded in the Western tradition and gives us a way to appreciate what the Buddha taught.

Further, not only is Jesus not expressing ill-will, he is actually praying that those who have performed these terrible acts won't be punished. "They know not what they do," means that they don't realize the karmic consequences of their behavior, which is probably true for many cruel and sadistic people.

The point of all this, though, is that perhaps practicing non–ill-will is more important than trying to be some model of sweetness and love. In fact, some people refer to the sort of behavior encountered at spiritual centers as "nicey-nice," that is, a phony love that doesn't have authentic kindness behind it. It's easy to put on a happy, spiritual demeanor in public, but our behavior at home (as described in chapter 2) or in our hearts is more telling.

The truth is we all contain the seeds of hatred and ill-will. Our challenge is to let go of those qualities. And what the Buddha's teachings imply is that when we abandon ill-will, what is left is loving-kindness. Perhaps it's less important that we try to cultivate love as it is that we abandon hate.

→ *reflection*
NON-ILL-WILL

The simile of the saw challenges us to let go of hatred. If we have been the victim of abuse or violence, or even if we simply see someone as creating harm in the world, it can be very difficult not to hold ill-will toward them. If we are trying to practice loving-kindness and the thought of such a person arises, how can we deal with that so as not to be swept away with negativity?

One approach is to reflect on karma; this is the foundation of the practice of equanimity, the fourth of the brahmaviharas. The Buddha says, "All beings are the owners of their karma," which means that whatever actions (thoughts, words, or deeds) they take will bear fruit of the same quality. Although we might not see the external results of this karma, we can trust that their inner life is poisoned by their own unskillful acts. When we see someone filled with hate, we remember how it feels to hate; when we see someone filled with greed, we remember how it feels to be caught in greed. These reflections can evoke compassion in us, seeing that because this person doesn't understand the law of karma, they don't realize that they are planting poisoned seeds in their own hearts and minds. We don't have to believe in rebirth to know that this karma will bring them suffering.

The other key reflection is observing how painful it is to be angry and resentful. This is what the Buddha emphasizes: that we are harming ourselves as much as our enemy with our anger; that we are giving our enemy what they want by creating suffering for ourselves.

Finally, perhaps the most difficult, but ultimately the most powerful practice is to send metta to our enemies. Understanding that all beings wish for happiness, even though they are often taking the exact wrong action to get it, we wish them happiness. This is often preceded by a forgiveness meditation (see below). Forgiveness helps us to gain perspective: to see how holding on to anger causes us suffering and to see that our enemy acted out of their own confusion and pain.

→ *practice*

FORGIVENESS

Forgiveness meditation starts by connecting with the heart:

Begin by settling into a comfortable posture where you can stay alert. Consciously relax with some deeper breaths, releasing any tension in the body.

Feel the breath in the center of the chest, the heart center, and have a sense of softening and opening in that place.

Once you've settled in for perhaps three to five minutes, begin to work with the three aspects of forgiveness: forgiving ourselves, forgiving others, and asking forgiveness.

- **Forgiving ourselves:** Begin by contemplating all the ways that you have harmed yourself, internally and externally. How have you talked to yourself or viewed yourself in negative terms? Self-hatred is a common condition in our culture, and as human beings, we don't deserve to be hated. Repeat these phrases to yourself: *For all the ways I have harmed myself through thought, word, and deed, I forgive myself. I forgive myself.* We may not feel anything right away, but it's important to stay with this process, and not just in a single sitting, but to keep coming back to this process over time until the tightness in the heart starts to break up and we begin to have a sense of self-forgiveness.
- **Forgiving others:** Anger harms us as much as it does our enemy. We are the ones who are living with the nagging thoughts and obsessions. To forgive others does not mean we condone their behavior or that we will ever let them hurt

The Simile of the Saw 55

us again. It just means that we don't want to carry this baggage with us. Bring to mind the people who have harmed you and the things they've done to you. Breathing into your heart, say to them, *For all the ways you have hurt me through thought, word, or deed, I offer my forgiveness. I forgive you.* Again, we can't expect instant results. But we need to stick with this process. Sometimes there will be a sudden shift or insight, and at others just a gradual melting of the icy heart. Stick with it.

- **Asking forgiveness:** Forgiveness meditation allows us to do the inner work of accepting forgiveness, whether or not we actually receive it externally. Bring to mind each person you've harmed, and say to yourself, *For all the ways that I hurt you, through thought, word, or deed, I ask your forgiveness. Please forgive me.* Again, it can be difficult to accept that we are forgiven, but this is a form of internal healing, admitting responsibility and asking if we can move on.

Work with these three aspects of forgiveness as much and for as long as is necessary. There's no timetable for forgiveness. You may find that you feel that one of the aspects really stands out as needing attention. That's fine. Use the practice in whatever ways feel beneficial to you.

four

A TROUBLED WORLD
The Greed, Hatred,
and Delusion Report

Sometimes when I'm reading or hearing the news, I feel as if my limbs are being sawed off. Maybe the news should be called "The Greed, Hatred, and Delusion Report." These are the three "poisons" that the Buddha says infect our lives. How to live happily in this atmosphere of conflict is one of the great challenges we face.

My practice opens me up so that I can't numb myself to the suffering of the refugee family drowning in the Mediterranean as they try to escape war and oppression; I can't escape the anger that arises when I see a Black man shot down in the street for a petty crime; I can't hold down my resentment at the CEO who walks away from a crumbling company with a golden parachute; and I can't restrain my disgust when I see advertisements that promise happiness with the purchase of a new car. But the Dharma tells me that I mustn't allow myself to be swept away by these feelings because if I do, I will be replicating the very qualities that I deplore. The peace activist who spits on the soldier returning from war acts on the same hatred that drives that war. As in *The Simile of the Saw*, the Buddha challenges us to take another way.

There are two things to consider when faced with the Greed, Hatred, and Delusion Report: my inner response and my outer response. On a daily basis, if I am going to be an engaged citizen, I must deal with all the feelings that arise around the Report, the anger, the wish to shut down, the resentment, fear, and disgust—and the heartbreak. At the same time I must consider how to respond in the world. Mindfulness and the brahmaviharas, the divine abodes, can offer some vital tools and guidelines for these considerations.

In Gil Fronsdal's translation of the famous fifth verse of the *Dhammapada*, the Buddha says, "Hatred never ends by hatred, but by non-hate alone does it end. This is an ancient truth." Cultivating loving-kindness gives us another way of responding to the hatred we see: with love and compassion, with joy and equanimity. These four brahmaviharas are the antidotes: love inside and love outside; compassion inside and compassion outside; joy inside and joy outside; equanimity inside and equanimity outside.

Love inside is the wish for all beings to be happy, whether they are kind or wise or not. This protects my own heart from the poison of hatred.

Love outside means my actions are motivated by love, even if that love is fiercely protective.

Compassion inside means I see my own agony when reading the Report, and I bring an attitude of kindness to myself; I also know that even the oppressor suffers, so I bring compassion to him or her as well. Thich Nhat Hanh's remarkable poem "Please Call Me by My True Names" expresses this compassion powerfully in evoking images of the Vietnamese boat people, a pirate who rapes a girl and the girl who is his victim. Both deserve our compassion he says. The pirate's heart is closed, his spirit crushed by war's brutality. He's so numb he can't even feel his own suffering. The girl's heart is broken as she throws herself into the sea, unable to live with the shame and trauma.

I try to think of this teaching when I see the cruelty on the front page. I try to remember that those who act hatefully and fearfully hold those very feelings within, carry hate and fear in their hearts every day. Even though I recoil from their actions, I remind myself that they are trapped in their own suffering, lost in a brutal worldview that plagues their minds and corrupts their entire lives. This is how I can arouse compassion for the dictators, exploiters, and oppressors of the world.

Perhaps the greatest challenge to compassion is our desire to turn away from other people's pain. I don't always give money to homeless people, but I do try to look them in the eye, to acknowledge them, both out of respect for their humanity and to see their suffering honestly. But the Report, with its worldwide scope, shows so much ordinary suffering that it can become overwhelming to take it all in. Hunger and oppression; addiction and disease; poverty and famine: with billions of people on our planet, it's inevitable that virtually every possible condition will be present. Besides, we have to recognize that the economics behind the business of producing the Report wants to emotionally trigger us in any way that will maintain our attention, just to keep the advertising dollars coming in. At some point, we have to protect ourselves compassionately by stepping back from all this information.

The point of understanding that the news is a Greed, Hatred, and Delusion Report is so that we *don't* have to read every detail of every story of misery. We already know the content of the news before we pick it up. The Buddha's teaching on the Middle Way suggests that we need to figure out how to be informed without being overwhelmed.

The next brahmavihara, joy, or mudita, offers us help.

Joy inside is the appreciation of life, even with its suffering. After all, why would we hold life so dear if it held no joy? When we discover the safety of the heart, the peace of the well-trained mind, and the beauty of pure awareness, we see that there's no need to add anything to life. It is inherently rich and fulfilling.

Joy outside is there in nature, in friends, and in love. It's in art and music, literature and film. The Report depicts a world riven by conflict and suffering, but if this were the whole of the story, it would hardly be a world worth saving. But we know this is only a part of the story, the part that gets our attention. Most of the moments of caring and connection, of generosity and sacrifice, of beauty and inspiration never make it into the Report. The Report tells us about the anomalies—the "man bites dog" stories—and never mentions that most people are living lives of peace, harmony, and love with their families and neighbors— and dogs. And so, the Report inflates the conflicts such that they gain outsize importance and significance.

The practice of joy reminds us to pay attention to the quieter events, the ones that more truly define our lives.

The fourth brahmavihara, equanimity, or upekkha, brings us balance and perspective, a peaceful, wise view of the world. This view is at the heart of the Buddhist understanding of the Greed, Hatred, and Delusion Report.

Upekkha has the special capacity to protect the other brahmaviharas so that love doesn't become foolish and blind; compassion doesn't burn out or shut down; and joy doesn't overload into mindless elation.

Equanimity inside comes from the mind training of meditation. The nervous system itself changes with deep practice, no longer so easily disturbed by thoughts and feelings, by fears or regrets. As an emotional person myself, someone who tends to fly high and then crash, equanimity is perhaps my most important protection. When I visit prisons to teach meditation, it's hard to see the misery of people locked up, deprived not only of their freedom, but of their identity. My compassion can lapse into pity and despair. In maximum security, even knowing that most of these men did very bad things, my own caring sometimes overwhelms me. I have to remind myself that I can only help them if I maintain my own balance and clarity. Here I try to call forth my clearest understanding of the Dharma, to transmit something pure and true, unfiltered by my emotionality or pity. I draw on my own years of practice to find a stable heart from which to speak.

Equanimity outside doesn't imply passivity or apathy. We still engage with politics or economics or any other social issue. We just do it with the larger understanding that there is no permanent solution to impermanent events; that no perfection exists in an imperfect world; that all humans are subject to the three poisons. As Buddhists we aren't putting ourselves above anyone or suggesting that we are different or better than anyone else, only that we have changed our view of the world and our intention to act in it. We at least want and hope to overcome the poisons, even if we fall short a good deal of the time.

At some point, though, we must simply accept all that we see in the Report. We can't control the world or the people in it. It's this realization that the Buddha expresses at times when someone refuses to understand his teaching: "Now is the time to do as you think fit."

While we can't control the world or correct every injustice, that doesn't mean we should just sit still and meditate as the world goes by. Buddhism may encourage pacifism, but not passivity. Western Buddhists have grappled with how to make their practice relevant for many years.

In the aftermath of the violence and disruption of the sixties, many people of my generation preferred to step away from society than to engage its ills. For those of us who treasured peace and nonviolence, both sides of the political divide—the establishment and the counterculture—offered unsatisfactory approaches to change. Our government had engaged in a futile, ruthless, and ill-founded war in Southeast Asia for over ten years, but the anti-war movement—at least its radicals—was characterized by hatred and violence of its own. Many of those, like myself, who sympathized with the goals of the anti-war movement, were alienated by its tactics, and so withdrew into a passive and disengaged stance.

A few Buddhists, though, saw a different way. They founded the Buddhist Peace Fellowship in 1978. Their goal was to bring together the insights they had gained from Buddhist practice with their sociopolitical consciousness. While for many years the work of these so-called "engaged" Buddhists was seen as something separate from what most meditators were doing, over time there has been a kind of merging of the contemplative and engaged streams of Western Buddhism.

This merging is probably most clearly embodied in Bhikkhu Bodhi, the translator of the Pali Canon. Here is a monk who spent decades in single-minded pursuit of making the vast collection of early Buddhist teachings available to a Western, English-speaking audience. The accomplishments of his scholarship and translations would, for an ordinary person, account for a lifetime's work—and a remarkable lifetime. However, over a decade ago, he found himself turning outward to address the suffering of the world directly.

Despite his preference for the peace of the contemplative life, he felt a growing responsibility to look for ways to be of practical service in the world. This drew him into founding an organization to address world hunger, Buddhist Global Relief. Taking the Buddha's words that "Hunger is the worst illness" as a guide, this nonprofit provides direct aid to people in many countries (and of many faiths), as well as helping develop ways for people to feed themselves through sustainable agriculture. In this work, they also discovered that educating girls had a significant benefit in reducing hunger, and so this became a second element of their project.

When I first heard of BGR and Bhikkhu Bodhi's role in founding it, I felt a kind of elation, a profound joy in learning that this hero of mine, someone whose translations had changed my world and the world of so many students of Buddhism, was pointing to the importance of a practice that was not simply inner-directed, but outer-directed as well.

In a 2007 article in *Lion's Roar* magazine, Bhikkhu Bodhi says we need to engage "conscientious compassion," based on "moral outrage." He elaborates on these strong words saying, "By 'moral outrage' I mean—not 'anger' as ordinarily understood—but a moral revulsion against policies, actions, and ideologies that violate the imperatives of justice, love, and peace, and entail dreadful harm for many people—a revulsion that compels one to engage in peaceful acts of resistance." If we are to take the Buddha's teachings on morality, nonviolence, and indeed on "greed, hatred, and delusion," seriously, then passivity in the face of morally outrageous actions is a betrayal of the mantel passed to us as his followers.

Each of us has our own path to follow, but what the Buddha—and Bhikkhu Bodhi—point to is that spiritual practice and the cultivation of loving-kindness are not simply personal projects. The insights that arise in this work carry with them a responsibility to our community and our world. Western Buddhists have tried to fulfill that responsibility in a number of areas, including broad issues of diversity, racism, sexism, and criminal justice.

How to create a more diverse sangha has been one of the ongoing challenges in Western Buddhism. I remember two decades ago looking around at one sitting group and realizing how white, straight, and middle class the whole group was. People started to call our path "the Upper Middle Way," an ironic play on the Buddha's description of his teaching. Talk started about how to be more inviting to people of color and the LGBTQ community who might not feel welcomed at our groups and centers. Spirit Rock Meditation Center, where I had trained and was teaching, initiated a diversity program, but in some ways, this felt like an add-on, something the center was trying to just patch onto the existing structure. It became clear that something different was needed, an entirely new center founded on the principles of diversity.

A small group of us—Black, Asian, gay, and white European—gathered for periodic discussions over a couple of years and tried to organize such a center. For me this was an opportunity for another awakening. I came to understand that the issues were far more complex than I had imagined, and I got to see some of my own bias and ignorance. Eventually we as a group realized that we didn't have the wherewithal to accomplish what we wanted together. We broke up, but the people of color and those from the LGBTQ community eventually picked up the pieces and put together the East Bay Meditation Center, EBMC, now a beacon in the Buddhist world, representative of the principles of love and inclusivity that the Dharma embodies.

In his own time, the Buddha addressed racism in the form of the caste system that defined people based on their family's position and role in society, not on their individual abilities or potential. When someone joined the Buddha's sangha as a monk or nun, they were considered to have become casteless. Just as they would leave all their possessions and their name behind, they would also abandon this class marker, a tool of oppression in India.

One of the first low-caste members to ordain with the Buddha was Upali, a barber from the Buddha's home village. He had followed some of the nobles who were planning to join the Buddha, and, in an act of humility, the nobles stepped aside to allow him to be ordained first so that this lowly worker would forever be their senior in the sangha.

In fact, over time Upali came to be recognized as the greatest authority on the monastic rules and after the Buddha's death was called upon to recite them at the First Council, the original gathering to codify the Buddha's teachings.

Setting aside caste in the Buddhist tradition has been picked up in modern times by the Indian reformer B. R. Ambedkar's Navayana ("New Vehicle") Buddhist movement, which promotes the conversion of Dalits—people belonging to the "untouchable" caste—to Buddhism so as to rid themselves of caste. The movement's conversion process involves a vow that explicitly rejects Hindu teachings while affirming faith in the Eightfold Path, taking refuge, and following the five precepts. Not surprisingly, these Dalit Indian Buddhists seem to be as interested in the Buddha's social and political efforts as his contemplative teachings.

Even as the Buddha openly welcomed every caste to the sangha, he hesitated to allow women to be ordained. It's disappointing to read how he at first refused to let his stepmother and other women from his home village take robes. Even after Ananda convinced him to change his mind, he predicted that their admission to the sangha would mean that his teachings wouldn't last as long, that they would be forgotten sooner. Perhaps he also had in mind situations like the one he eventually faced with Moliya Phagguna being overly interested in the nuns.

Even though he did bring women into the monastic sangha, their history as members has not been easy. At one point the lineage of nuns in the Theravada tradition died out, and the monks used this as an excuse to lower the status of women who came later to ordination. This condition continues in Asian Theravada countries today so that a monk who was ordained yesterday has preferential status to a woman who has been a nun for ten years. As you can imagine, many Western nuns find this sort of discrimination totally unacceptable, and in order to get around the technical rules set down by Theravada monks, some of these nuns have taken a second ordination in the Mahayana tradition, which doesn't have the same strictures as the Theravada.

One of these ordinations took place at my home center, Spirit Rock, in Northern California. The words and images from that day in 2011 speak to the values of engaged, modern Buddhism: the nuns walking side by side (not behind) the monks; the ordination in a circle that represents equality and unity; monastics attending and witnessing from across traditions, Theravada and Mahayana, Western and Asian; and laypeople—Asian, African American, and white—basking in the glow of this joyous occasion.

Another Buddhist social justice project involves taking meditation into prisons. When I took part in teaching a day-long retreat at a maximum-security facility, I was impressed by the sincerity of the inmates as they practiced and discussed the Dharma. I looked at them in their bland prison uniforms and envisioned their monotonous lives and felt grief for their misery. Only at the end of the day, when I was told that one of the most engaged participants was a lifer who'd been a paid killer, murdering competing drug dealers for money, did I realize that my compassion, while well-intended, might be somewhat naive. While I understood that he, too, was subject to suffering, and that the conditions of his life had very likely been pretty awful, I also understood that it was best for society, and perhaps for him as well, that he be in prison—a painful realization.

So-called "stupid" compassion doesn't take into account the actual situation. Anagarika Munindra, the Indian Buddhist teacher of Joseph Goldstein, Sharon Salzberg, and many other Westerners, was famous for his practical teachings. One day Sharon came back to the temple, upset and shaken, to report that she'd been assaulted by a man who tried to drag her off a rickshaw. While she had escaped serious harm, she didn't know how to respond, because she thought that as a Buddhist she wasn't supposed to get angry. Munindra told her, "With all the loving-kindness in your heart you should have taken your umbrella and hit that man over the head."

While I laughed at Munindra's turn of phrase, I also learned something important, that compassion has to be balanced with wisdom—that I can act assertively while still maintaining peace within. This expresses the essence of engaged Buddhism, balancing a loving and peaceful heart with a determination to resist injustice.

The Buddha's path demands that we look deeply inside, that we awaken peace, wisdom, and compassion in our hearts. And then it inspires us to bring these qualities out of our hearts and into the world. Each of us must discover for ourselves what this means, what our special part is in sharing the transformative insights of the Dharma.

→ *reflection*

READING THE GREED, HATRED, AND DELUSION REPORT

From time to time when engaging with the news, reflect on whether the story you are hearing is one of greed, hatred, or delusion. Greed takes many forms: unfair tax laws, corporate takeovers, offshore banking, and many others. Hatred appears in war and other acts of violence, racism, religious bias, and more. Delusion often appears in advertising products promising happiness or peace. All three can blend together in ways that make them indistinguishable.

As you read or watch these stories see if you can develop what Venerable Analayo calls "inner distancing," just watching these destructive expressions of human nature as if you were a scientist or alien visiting from a sane planet. Remember, human history is virtually defined by these poisons. There's nothing new under the sun.

→ *reflection*

ENGAGED PRACTICE

During one of your meditation periods, take some time to reflect on your spiritual values and how you might live them more fully in the world. Is there a community group, activist organization, or other volunteer activity that you might join? Does your sangha have any outreach opportunities? Or perhaps look closer to home, like an elderly neighbor who could use help or local school that needs volunteers. Finding ways to express "living kindness" takes our practice out of the personal and theoretical and challenges us to integrate our beliefs more fully into our lives.

five

BORN FROM THOSE WHO ARE DEAR
Nonattachment

Even as the Buddha extols the importance of loving everyone—ourselves, our dear ones, even our enemies—he warns against the risk of another kind of love: that founded in need, attachment, and clinging. Ironically, though the *Metta Sutta* uses mother love as the ideal image of loving-kindness, it's parental attachment that he uses to explain this danger.

I stumbled on this idea in my early, somewhat random exploration of the suttas in the Majjhima Nikaya. With my daughter still a toddler, I wondered if the Buddha had any teachings about the joy or at least the experience of parenthood. Paging through the table of contents, I found a sutta entitled *Born from Those Who Are Dear* (MN 87) and thought, "Perfect! This will be something about the beauty of the parent-child relationship." Wrong. (Is it only a coincidence that this sutta follows *On Angulimala*, the story of a serial killer?)

In the Buddha's typical, unsentimental way, the sutta points out all the suffering that happens when we are emotionally attached to others. This was not the message I wanted to read, as I was in the throes of deep attachment to my daughter. But reading the sutta, I had to admit that the Buddha was right (as usual).

The sutta begins by telling us about a man whose only son has died. He is inconsolable and wanders around crying, "My only child, where are you?" When he goes to the Buddha, probably hoping for some words of comfort, the Buddha first tells him that his "faculties are deranged," not exactly a kindly message. The father asks, "How could my faculties not be deranged" considering the circumstances? And here's where the Buddha delivers his message: "Sorrow, lamentation, pain, grief, and despair are born from those who are dear, arise from those who are dear."

The father remains unconvinced, saying that "happiness and joy are born from those who are dear," and he leaves the Buddha "displeased." Now he encounters some gamblers nearby, and when he tells them of this interchange, they agree that the Buddha has got it all wrong, that our loved ones bring us happiness, not pain. "I agree with the gamblers," says the man.

One thing we can be sure of in the suttas, if you agree with gamblers in opposition to the Buddha, then you are definitely on the wrong track.

The story of this encounter gets back to the palace where our friends King Pasenadi and Queen Mallika, who told each other they loved themselves, hear it. Mallika, being the Buddha's devotee, says that it must be true if the Buddha says so. Pasenadi, perhaps a bit jealous, seems to mock her devotion, saying that no matter what the Buddha says she agrees, just like an apple-polishing student.

The queen wants to make sure she has it right and sends a Brahmin to confirm what the Buddha said. When he does so,

Mallika goes to Pasenadi and asks how he would feel if the princess got ill or died. He admits that he would suffer terribly. She then lists other people he loves and gets the same response. Finally she asks how he'd feel if something happened to some of the regions he ruled. For those of us who aren't rulers, this might be similar to our house burning down or our car being stolen. At this point Pasenadi gets it, that suffering arises from his attachment to that which is dear.

This teaching comes right out of the second noble truth, that the cause of suffering is clinging—even clinging to loved ones. And yet, it still comes as a surprise—at least it did to me. I understood it, it made sense, and I had lived it, but still it just seemed so stark and unforgiving. Wasn't there anything else the Buddha would say to comfort us? Something about love or family or just being human? Not in this sutta.

The focus throughout the sutta is the suffering people experience when one of their beloved family members dies. But it certainly doesn't take death for us to be dismayed with our beloveds. In fact, many parents struggle with their children's life choices; family members get into bitter quarrels; lovers break each other's hearts; friends betray friends; and parents neglect children who depend on them. People we don't care about have much less effect on our feelings than those we love. Of course, there are exceptions, like an unfair boss or an abusive police officer. But our daily lives and emotions are more intertwined with "those who are dear," and those relationships can put a great deal of strain on us.

When you hear this teaching, you might think, "I guess that means I shouldn't be attached to anyone." But I don't think this is the message. After all, attachment to dear ones is practically impossible to avoid in life. Did the Buddha think we should sever all human relationships and live alone? Perhaps if we look at his life superficially, we could make that assessment. After all, he left his own wife, child, and parents to pursue enlightenment. But eventually he came back and tried to teach them the Dharma as well, even ordaining his own son, Rahula. The fact that more than one sutta was given directly to Rahula suggests that his son had a special place in his life.

And even as he lived as a wandering ascetic, the Buddha formed relationships, first with two teachers, and later with five other seekers. After his enlightenment, his first impulse was to return to his teachers and share what he had learned—surely a sign that he cared about them. When he realized they had died, he sought out his five ascetic friends and taught them the Dharma.

Over his lifetime he formed deep bonds with some of his followers and companions on the path. In his old age when his two senior disciples, Sariputta and Moggallana, passed away within weeks of each other, he said the sangha seemed "empty" to him. Clearly he had feelings of affection for them. But he didn't despair or lose his mind about that loss, saying that it was "wonderful" and "amazing" that he experienced "no sorrow or lamentation." In SN 47.14, he explains that it would make no sense that "what is born, come to be, conditioned, and subject to disintegration not disintegrate," so why should we be disturbed by this reality?

In the same way, when he approached his own death, he told his followers not to despair at his passing, that they should keep the Dharma as their refuge. What all these teachings are pointing to is acceptance of impermanence and the wisdom that comes from that acceptance. The Buddha distinguishes pain—in this case, the pain of loss—from suffering, "sorrow, lamentation," and so on. When he tells the grieving father that his faculties are deranged, he's talking about keeping perspective, understanding what is true, seeing things through the lens of wisdom, not that he shouldn't be sad. With this perspective, it's not that we don't mourn, but there's no confusion in that mourning. Understanding that love and loss are natural parts of human existence profoundly shifts how we experience them. When they come as a surprise or we don't understand why they are happening, we can get overwhelmed with grief. But when we have this understanding that everything that arises must also pass away, we can accept loss, even if it's painful.

Parenting is a perfect opportunity to reflect on these teachings. Nothing bad has to happen to your child to experience a sense of loss over time. The joy and delight of an infant are lost when they begin to walk and talk; the toddler's triumphs are soon left behind by the preschooler; and before we know it, instead of a child that worships us, we are dealing with a surly, resentful teenager. And then she is gone.

We don't have to be a parent to experience this kind of loss. Most people outlive their own parents and must live through that loss. Other dear ones pass away. And even short of death, who hasn't lost a friend? We move, we grow apart, our lives diverge. Life is change, and yet our hearts and minds want to hold on. This is the fundamental mistake that drives us. Underneath dukkha there is always this element of wanting to hold on or wanting to control. Even as we wake up to the truth, this pull remains.

While parental love is a deep kind of attachment, romantic love, underpinned by sexual attraction, presents a whole other kind of clinging. This is a challenging issue to address through Buddhist teachings. Those teachings came from a celibate man who encouraged his core followers to lead a celibate monastic life as well. Yet as the Dharma has come to the West, it's largely been laypeople who have pursued the ideal of enlightenment the Buddha put forth. By forgoing the monastic discipline and celibacy, we are forced to confront different challenges than the monastics. The way I understand it, enlightenment is more easily achieved for monastics simply because there are fewer distractions and more opportunities for a committed practice. This isn't to say that celibate monastics don't continue to have sexual feelings. I have heard some of them talk about this as part of their practice. But by not acting on those feelings they certainly create fewer emotional complications in their lives.

While we don't have to look at either celibacy or lay life as good or bad, we should recognize how things work and take responsibility for our decisions. I'm convinced that the monastic life is more conducive to enlightenment, and I see a real beauty in sexual renunciation. I also see that it wasn't something I could take on in this lifetime.

It's important to be realistic in talking about these spiritual teachings, or else we get caught in a cycle of self-judgment and a sense of failure as we try to live up to unattainable ideals. Repressing, ignoring, or hiding our sexual energy rarely works out well. Many spiritual communities have been shattered when the (usually male) leaders have been exposed as sexually exploiting their (usually female) students. This happens when the teacher puts forth an ideal that he's not willing or able to live up to. (I don't want to go into the sexual abuse scandals in the Catholic Church, but they certainly relate to this issue.)

So, if you have decided that you aren't going to be celibate, but you are serious about your spiritual practice, what are you to do? First of all, I would say be honest with yourself about your sexuality. Don't repress, ignore, or hide it. At the same time, you need to find a way to live in harmony with the basic precepts of non-harming. For most people, this will mean monogamy, though there are people and communities (I live in the Bay Area) for whom multiple sexual partners is acceptable. To me, as long as people are open and honest about these issues and are willing to accept the consequences of their actions, then that's their choice.

Here we come back to the Buddha's most basic question: Is your attachment causing suffering? As a young man, lust had a big part in my decision-making and in my actions. My relationships were initiated from feelings of lust; when that lust subsided, conflict often arose; infidelity due to lust created more conflicts; and, despite this persistent effort to satisfy my desires, I was never satisfied.

As I got older and started to understand these patterns and change my behaviors, my relationships became healthier and more long-lasting, until eventually I got married. But it would be dishonest, silly even, to say I wasn't sexually attracted to my wife. Lust was still involved in my attraction to her—to state the obvious. What I'm getting at is that, for the layperson, perfect nonattachment is simply not realistic, and setting that as a goal will actually cause another kind of suffering, the suffering of self-judgment.

This dilemma brings us to a crossroads in our understanding of the Buddha's teachings. Do we strive for and measure ourselves against the perfection of the enlightened one, or do we accept some lesser standard? There are risks in both: judging ourselves is just another form of attachment, but setting lower standards can be a way to escape responsibility for our shortcomings. We have to bring the rigorous honesty of mindfulness to examine our true intentions. When we look at the underlying impulses this examination reveals and then see how those impulses condition the results of our actions, we'll gain more clarity. If our relationships keep creating conflict or pain for us or our partner, then something is askew. If we find we can sustain relative harmony and comfort, then we likely have a found a good balance.

I'm not going to tell you that I have the answer to these conundrums, only that I have come to (relative) peace with my own decisions. Buddhism doesn't so much tell us how to live our lives as it gives us tools for finding our own way to happiness.

One of the ways that we fool ourselves into thinking we are acting skillfully in our intimate relationships is when we are caught by what Buddhism calls "near enemies." Near enemies are things that look like or seem like other positive qualities, but are actually not useful.

The near enemy of loving-kindness is desire. As I was driven by lust in my twenties, I thought it was based in love. "I love you" often meant, "I'm sexually attracted to you." That desire leads us to act in a kind and loving way, so it's masquerading as metta, but what's behind it, the intention, is to satisfy desire. This can then result in something very different from the expression of metta. When the demands and expectations of desire aren't satisfied, our so-called love can turn into something ugly: obsession, jealousy, and even hatred. The irony of the lover who murders his beloved is the most tragic outcome of this near enemy, but a great deal of other suffering has come from confusing desire with love.

A near enemy of compassion is pity. Where compassion is "feeling with," pity doesn't have the "with," but keeps us separated from the one who is struggling. Instead of truly caring about someone, we see them as different from us, the one with a problem. In an intimate relationship this undermines the whole sense of connection and can set up a relationship of dependency, as the "well" person takes care of the "suffering" one. This then easily moves into the near enemy of sympathetic joy, codependence.

Codependence is the *need* for others to be happy in order to feel happy ourselves. This kind of caring neglects the self in order to take care of others. It ignores the first step of metta meditation: cultivating love for oneself. Without this practice for yourself, you can't actually love others in an authentic way; your love will always be tainted by self-hatred or self-judgment. The love you are expressing is essentially a desire for others to make you feel okay about yourself, a messy equation that says, if I love you enough and take care of you, then you will love me back and make me feel okay about myself. There are many ways that this doesn't work: first of all, the object of your love will often feel smothered by your efforts to take care of them; second, even if they return your care, the nature of codependence, like addiction, is that it can never be satisfied. This is essentially a kind of love addiction, an insatiable grasping after affection.

So, we can see that codependence is "born from those who are dear." Not that those who are dear are to blame, but rather that the way we relate to those we love can be codependent.

The near enemy to equanimity is apathy or numbness. We look as if we are peaceful, but we're actually emotionally shut down. In trying to be detached we can become blinkered to the world. As we find peace in meditation, we can become attached to that quietude and not want to come out of that safe cocoon into feeling the fullness of life's challenges.

The brahmaviharas interact to protect each other from the near enemies. Loving-kindness, compassion, and joy protect equanimity by keeping us open to our emotions and our capacity to be touched; compassion protects loving-kindness and joy from overlooking suffering, dukkha; sympathetic joy brings balance to the suffering we see in compassion; and equanimity protects the other three from becoming overwhelmed with emotion. This is especially true of equanimity's relationship to compassion: as we engage the world's pain and try to bring care and kindness, we can easily burn out or become depressed and despairing. Upekkha, the quality of equanimity, helps us maintain the broader perspective of Dharma: that although all conditioned things are impermanent and unsatisfactory—subject to dukkha—if we avoid clinging and aversion we can still find meaning and happiness in life. Here we see the Buddha's Middle Way in action, creating a balance between openness and inner peace, between engagement and detachment.

While suffering may be born from those who are dear, it's also possible to see how grief can transmute into spiritual awakening. I saw this in a stark and powerful way when, a month before my daughter graduated from high school, one of her classmates drowned on an excursion in the Sierras. Even though he wasn't a personal friend of hers, our family, like many in her large high school, felt deeply touched by the loss. The turnout for his memorial filled the big courtyard at the center of campus. Quietly the crowd examined the sprawling sheets of butcher-block paper that were laid out for people to record their remembrances of this vivacious teenager. There was a rare sense of the sacred in the air, teenagers whispering to each other, gentle tears flowing, and a feeling of shared grief. Every parent, no matter whether they had known this boy or not, felt the stinging loss his parents felt. Every student felt the loss his friends felt.

I could sense that something more than grief was happening. This was not just sorrow, but also a waking up to the preciousness of life.

And one other thing struck me: during the entire ceremony I never saw anyone look at a cell phone. Here were hundreds of teenagers whose lives seem to hinge on their relationships to their phones, completely letting go of that habit. No one told them to, there were no signs or rules. It was a natural part of their arriving in the present moment, the moment of love, compassion, and appreciation that the memorial called forth. The speeches and remembrances of that afternoon expressed much more joy in life than despair in loss. We were all being given a reminder of what is most valuable in our lives.

The Buddha often talked about grief. In another famous story from the commentaries, a woman, Kisa Gotami, is overwhelmed with the death of her baby boy. She comes to the Buddha with his lifeless body begging him to bring her child back to life. The Buddha tells her that he will do so if she can simply bring a mustard seed from any house in the village that has not experienced loss. As she goes desperately from house to house, she learns that everyone has lost a parent or child, an uncle or aunt, a grandparent, sibling, or cousin, that no family is free from loss. Insight into impermanence arises in her and she awakens, joining the Buddha's community as a nun.

Death, loss, and the realization of impermanence have forever been spiritual teachers. Just as the cancer diagnosis so often wakes people up to the preciousness of this present moment, so Kisa Gotami's understanding that nothing can be held on to freed her from the overwhelming suffering of her loss. We live in the illusion of safety and stability, sleepwalking through the routines of daily life, following the dictates of society and inner craving. For many of us, only when we are hit by some crisis, shocked by devastating events, do we wake up to what we already know: life is short; bodies and minds are fragile; everything is temporary and insubstantial. That wake-up is a precious reminder to appreciate this very moment and the love that we can give and receive while we are alive.

The Buddha didn't say there was something wrong or unwise about feeling a connection with others. He simply reminded us that these connections were fragile, like life itself, and if we expected that they would never change, we were in for a deep disappointment.

One of the special elements of Buddhist teachings is how every challenge in life offers an opportunity for waking up. Sickness, old age, and death can be doors to wisdom; sorrow, anger, and fear can be mindfulness bells; a flat tire or a leaking roof can be a reminder of impermanence—no experience is wasted or useless. It's up to us, though, to make the most of life and its myriad gateways to freedom. In fact, one well-known chant, which begins "all things are impermanent," concludes by saying that understanding this truth brings joy. One might ask, "How does understanding that everyone dies, that everything changes, that you can't hold on to anything make someone *happy?*"

Perhaps consider the alternative: not understanding or accepting impermanence. This puts us in more or less constant conflict with reality. The car breaks down, the computer crashes, the toilet backs up; the stock market drops, your political party loses power, you're laid off from your job. All of these events can be viewed as mistakes, abnormal disruptions of how life is "supposed" to be. And with that view, we struggle with fear and anger, with despair and confusion. How would we experience these things if instead of these reactions, our thought was, "This is impermanence! The Dharma unfolding!"

I'm not suggesting that we can be absolutely serene as the toilet overflows and our job disappears, but when we understand such events as natural—rather than as cracks in the universe—our experience is vastly different.

Perhaps our most difficult struggle with change is with our own body. When we look in the mirror, impermanence is looking back. Aging is just dying in slow motion, and death is the ultimate loss for the individual. People try to pretend it's not happening with face-lifts and hair dyes, makeup and youthful outfits. We try to forestall it by living a healthy lifestyle, exercising and eating all the right foods. Beneath all these behaviors is dukkha, trying to hold on to life, to youth.

It's part of the Buddha's brilliant and counterintuitive teachings that accepting loss, even that of our most beloved child, can be a doorway to awakening. We can't hold on, not to our computer or our money, to our child or our own lives. The only way to be free is to live in harmony with this truth.

→ *reflection*

NONATTACHMENT

Take some time on your own, with a partner, or with a group to consider and discuss the implications of the *Born from Those Who Are Dear* sutta in your own life. Where does suffering arise because of emotional attachment? Does it even seem possible or reasonable to *not* be attached to loved ones? How do you manage those feelings and conflicts?

six

AS A MOTHER PROTECTS HER CHILD
Living Fearlessly

The origins of the practice of loving-kindness and the *Metta Sutta* are recorded in the commentaries to the Suttanipata. As the story goes, a group of monks went off to meditate in a forest. There the "tree spirits" or devas resented the monks' intrusion into their space and set about spooking them. These devas managed to terrify the monks and completely disrupt their concentration, sending them running back to the Buddha for help. I'm not sure that I believe in tree spirits (though I think trees themselves *are* spirits), but I can relate to how scary it can be to sleep out in the woods.

This is when the Buddha taught the monks the *Metta Sutta*, telling them that it would both help them to concentrate and protect them from any demons. When the monks took the sutta and its practice back to the forest, the devas were so moved by the love radiating from the monks that they not only accepted them sitting among their trees, but actively took care of them while they meditated.

Whether taken literally or as myth, the story has the same meaning: love is the antidote to fear. It protects us. When we are able to respond with love, fear is conquered.

How does metta address our fear?

Metta is the practice of openness and non-separation. It asks us to risk letting down the walls, thinking of the welfare of others instead of ourselves. In short, it tells us that protecting the illusory self is not the way to freedom. Metta is not only a practice to *cultivate* fearlessness, but an expression of the *wisdom* of fearlessness. Understanding metta means understanding the truth of interdependence and the insubstantiality of self.

How, then, to practice fearless metta? As with all Buddhist practice, the starting point is mindfulness, in this case, mindfulness of fear. Our tendency is often to avoid feeling difficult emotions or addressing them head-on. Instead of being with our feelings, we tend to either react to them or try to suppress or overcome them—fight or flight.

Buddhism offers a third way: awareness, openness, investigation, and acceptance. These are the key components of mindfulness. With fear, this means a willingness to first and foremost feel the uncomfortable quality of this emotion. In practical terms, this means allowing the fear to arise and flow through our body and mind without resistance. The breath anchors us in the present moment and helps the fearful energy move through the body. As we become more intimate with this feeling, we bring an attitude of caring and kindness—metta—to the feeling itself. We try to soothe our own fear with this attitude. Soon we may find that we are able to let go of many of the common manifestations of fear in a natural, effortless way.

If it's true, as the title of the seventies self-help book proclaims, that *Love Is Letting Go of Fear*, then that must mean *hate* is clinging to fear. As simplistic as this formula may appear, it holds a basic truth.

I learned this lesson many years ago when I worked for a delivery service in LA. The days were long and stressful driving my beat-up Subaru down crowded boulevards and highways shuttling documents and packages to law offices, banks, and other businesses around the city. One late afternoon coming down the Hollywood Freeway after my last delivery, traffic tight but still moving fast, a car weaving across lanes suddenly cut in front of me, forcing me to slam on the brakes and swerve to avoid an accident. The driver kept right on going, while I felt a rush of anger grab hold. Exhausted, caffeinated, and edgy I jumped on the gas and went after him. Caught in the grip of my rage, I came up on him and did the same thing he did to me, swerving in front of him and narrowly avoiding an accident. He leaned on his horn and cut across lanes again, disappearing amid the mass of cars approaching downtown LA.

My heart pounding, my head swimming now, I pulled off the highway onto the shoulder, still holding fast to the steering wheel. I sat there taking deep breaths and trying to calm down. What was I thinking? I could have gotten killed! What if that guy had a gun? I knew I'd been terribly foolish, but I didn't really understand why I'd reacted that way.

When someone cuts us off on the highway, they are endangering our lives. Even though we may not think of it that way consciously, our body and our nervous system know it. That danger triggers fear. What our bodies and minds often do with that fear is turn it into anger. Our survival instinct tells us that if we are in danger, we need to protect ourselves—and that very often means we need to fight. As though we were being attacked, we go into an aggressive mode. We are operating a large machine that can be a violent weapon, and we are in a sense trapped on the road. In the logic of fight or flight, there's no real room for flight, so fight it is.

This process plays out in many ways that have broader implications than a dangerous moment in our cars.

Fear of change, fear of "the other," fear of losing power or wealth or land, these are all drivers of hatred, the motors behind war, oppression, and exploitation. Human history is littered with the rubble of these fears, and our own era continues this tragic pattern. The roots of these horrors lie in the fear and hatred that live in the human mind. As we as individuals hate, so too do our communities and nations. No amount of treaties or international agreements can eliminate the roots of war.

Only the transformation of human consciousness will change the larger human culture. It is this transformation that Buddhism seeks.

While fear can trigger anger when we are physically threatened, ego threats can have similar results. This often plays out in our most intimate relationships.

Once when I was returning from a ten-day retreat, my then girlfriend (now wife) picked me up at the airport. We had plans to attend a party. I was in the throes of post-retreat bliss and started blathering about going on more retreats, longer retreats, and on and on. Rosemary wasn't pleased with the idea of my disappearing for long periods of time. That wasn't her idea of a relationship, and she let me know how frustrating it was to hear what I was saying.

I blew up, immediately going into a defensive mode, telling her that's who I was, so she'd have to deal with it. We never made it to the party.

All Rosemary was saying was that she wanted to have a partner who was around, not spending months at a time away on retreat, but I took it as an "attack," some kind of threat to my identity. That so-called attack then triggered fear in me that came out as anger.

I know I'm not the only person who's grown defensive and angry in a conflict with their partner. In these relationships our openness expresses the longing of the human heart to be known on the deepest level, to connect, even to merge with another. But when the passion and romance of falling in love begin to fade a bit, we can find ourselves emotionally vulnerable in ways we weren't prepared for.

When some disagreement or conflict then arises, we have the sense that we are being threatened on a very basic level. Now the trigger for conflict is set off. One person might emotionally withdraw or shut down while the other demands more love, more closeness. Both reactions come out of fear. We feel our ego is under attack, and that fear triggers anger.

The Buddha's teaching on selflessness points a path through this. Instead of seeing our thoughts and feelings as personal, we come to understand them as simply momentary manifestations of the mind. We step back from our reactive emotions and ask ourselves how real, or indeed, how important they are. In an intimate relationship, we have to consider what truly matters to us: being "right" or being together. We remember to call forth the love that forms the basis of our connection. In that moment, the fear and defensiveness recede, and we are drawn back into caring and mutual appreciation.

Whether on the global level or in these most intimate human bonds, the relationship between fear and anger points to why the Buddha taught loving-kindness as an antidote to fear.

Anxiety, the subtle and pervasive cousin of fear, underlies a broad swath of other feelings and behaviors. While fear, is often sudden and obvious, quickly coming and going, anxiety can run like a background hum through our lives. It's a sense that something isn't right, that we aren't safe, or that there is something wrong with us. It can manifest as impatience or irritability, elation or distraction. Under the influence of anxiety people overeat, overwork, and drive too fast. They spend too much and obsess about anything that will take their mind off their feelings and fears. They try to control things that are beyond their control.

To reflect on love and the sense of safety and comfort that love brings is the antidote to anxiety. When we wish ease and happiness for ourselves, we enter a realm of peace; when we wish it for others, we take ourselves out of our self-centered world and into the spaciousness of metta.

Anxiety can open us to the reality that life itself is not secure. The title of Alan Watts's book *The Wisdom of Insecurity* points to this other view, that what we are feeling actually makes sense. After all, life always ends with death, so we will inevitably lose everything. Watts is suggesting in this title that understanding this truth doesn't have to be a problem, but actually a way to free ourselves from a limited and ultimately failed view of reality. As long as we think we will someday find real safety and security in the world, we will always be caught in this fruitless search, strung along by an illusion that only creates more confusion, stress, and agitation. Opening to the ultimate reality that all things must pass is the wisdom that brings true relief.

→ *practice*

BREATHING WITH FEAR

To practice with fear we need a strong willingness. Our instinct is to avoid, so we need to be committed to the process. The practice focuses on body sensations and experiences, avoiding entanglements of the mind. Try applying it next time you are anxious or afraid.

Start with several deeper breaths and relaxing the body.

Feel the fear as sensation and energy in the body.

Give space for those sensations, releasing any tendency to suppress or hold back.

Keep breathing and releasing.

Relax the facial muscles, jaw, forehead, eyes.

Relax the shoulders.

Relax the belly.

Continue to feel the energy, noticing any tendency to tighten or resist.

Continue to relax and breathe.

If anxiety starts to get stronger, take more deep breaths and slowly exhale, releasing tension.

Notice the thoughts behind the fear and recognize their emptiness.

You are alive; you are breathing; trust that you can hold these feelings with kindness and wisdom.

seven

SUSTAIN THIS RECOLLECTION
Mindfulness and Metta

A superficial understanding of metta meditation would make you think it had nothing to do with mindfulness. In combining thoughts like "May you be happy" with images of the people we are sending metta to, we are operating in a mental realm, not focusing on the present moment or on reality. If you don't understand this practice in the context of the broader teachings, it can seem like fantasizing, just hoping for things to happen, or even believing that you are making those things happen. Either way, you're falling into the hindrance of desire.

It doesn't help that mindfulness and loving-kindness are usually taught as separate exercises. Just as on my first retreat loving-kindness was offered in the crowning moment near the close, on virtually every retreat I've attended, periods of loving-kindness meditation have been set aside as something different from the standard insight and mindfulness periods. Unless the retreat is explicitly a metta retreat, mindfulness is usually given primacy, the instruction given in the morning, while metta falls to an afternoon or early evening slot. I confess that I often follow the same format in my own retreats.

A few lines from the suttas, such as the key *Satipatthana Sutta* (MN 10) on the foundations of mindfulness, point us to the connection between mindfulness and loving-kindness. The Buddha begins the *Satipatthana Sutta* by declaring, "Bhikkhus, this is the direct path for the purification of beings, for the surmounting of sorrow and lamentation, for the disappearance of pain and grief... namely, the four foundations of mindfulness." Surmounting sorrow and grief and overcoming inner pain speak to the same goal and effect of brahmavihara practice. The love, compassion, appreciation, and emotional balance cultivated with metta practices address these very challenges. And in another of the foundational teachings, the *Anapanasati Sutta* (MN 118), the Buddha's discourse on mindfulness of breathing, the Buddha says a practitioner should "breathe in, gladdening the mind," pointing to the pleasant qualities associated with mindfulness.

In the *Metta Sutta*, we're told to wish "in gladness and in safety, may all beings be at ease," drawing a straight line to the *Anapanasati* instructions. Further on in the *Metta Sutta*, we are told to "sustain this recollection," or in Bhikkhu Bodhi's translation, "resolve on this mindfulness," showing that mindfulness must be there in order to successfully practice metta.

These lines of connection give us clarity about how mindfulness and loving-kindness are connected. Digging into the actual practices, we can see how this plays out.

If you look first at metta practice, it becomes pretty apparent that it won't go far without mindfulness. As I've cataloged, the obstructions to loving-kindness, from self-judgment to anger and fear, must all be seen clearly before any significant degree of metta can be aroused. And this seeing requires mindfulness.

Even the start of metta practice, connecting with the breath in the heart, is a form of mindfulness. Modern mindfulness teachers guide people to feel the breath at the nostrils or the belly. The heart just happens to sit right between the two. This idea of a "heart practice," is often characterized as metaphorical, and yet the connection to the body is real. Love is felt in the body, and while the organ that pumps our blood may not be its seat, for some reason, that area of the chest seems to be a place where this emotion is felt, in both a physical and emotional sense.

After centering awareness in the body, the Buddha's instructions on mindfulness move to the mind: our thoughts, feelings, and reactivity. These mental experiences can subtly influence our practice. For example, if we aren't aware that we're irritable or anxious, we might not understand why we're struggling to arouse metta. Once we realize the difficulty is because of our mood, we can be less judgmental of ourselves, and even bring some metta to the feelings. When the Buddha tells Moliya Phagguna he must maintain a mind of loving-kindness no matter how the bhikkhunis are abused, he's telling him that he must watch the reactions in his mind and abandon any thoughts of anger. Again, mindfulness is the precondition to loving-kindness.

Mindfulness can also point up our biases and the limits of our capacity to love. This became clear to me some years ago while working at a tech company in San Francisco. I had crafted a metta practice that I hoped would be relevant to my daily life. Every morning while walking from the subway to my office, I sent metta to each person I passed, silently repeating "May you be happy." On the crowded sidewalks of downtown San Francisco, this meant that I was constantly and rapidly repeating the phrase. As I walked, I passed businesspeople in suits, other tech workers in khakis, tattooed hipsters with messenger bags on their shoulders, and homeless people with their hands out. Young and old, tall and short, every race and class: a cross section of humanity.

There was a certain joy in this indiscriminate spreading of love, and it helped me connect with the Buddha's admonition to "radiate kindness over the entire world." But something else struck me as well as I walked up Second Street, headed for Folsom. Despite my attempt to radiate kindness equally to everyone I passed, my mind, just as rapidly, made a judgment and showed a preference with virtually each person: a certain aversion to the bankers and lawyers, attraction to the young women, disgust at some of the filthy homeless, and disinterest in large slices of people. This realization that my metta practice was biased resulted from the mindfulness that was accompanying the metta. Mindfulness, I was finding out, is an essential partner to metta.

When we practice metta meditation, we must be careful. It's easy to slip into a variety of counterproductive states. One of these is longing: as we think of people we love we can get lost in nostalgia or sentimentality, which distracts from the unconditional nature of metta. Another state is aversion, which can happen when we think of the difficult person. It's quite a challenge, in fact, to maintain balance at that stage of practice. Finally, it's easy to space out when working with the neutral person, just getting bored. In all of these cases, mindfulness needs to accompany the metta practice to keep us on track, to help us "sustain this recollection."

Outside of formal metta practice, mindfulness helps us respond with kindness, compassion, and balance. Although we might think that living kindness means trying to be "nice" in every situation, that's not always the wisest course of action. Applying metta to the complexities of life requires judgment and discrimination, which are founded in mindfulness. For instance, many homeless advocates encourage people to support shelters rather than give cash directly to people on the street who might spend it on drugs or alcohol. While the kind action might seem to be handing a dollar to a person who is clearly suffering, wisdom tells us something different. In the same way, I've often had to advise parents of addicts to stop supporting their children because that "kindness" was only perpetuating their addiction, allowing them to avoid facing the true costs of their behavior.

But while we can see that mindfulness is part of metta, is metta truly part of mindfulness? Mindfulness is often presented as a sort of neutral state, something disconnected from feelings of love or compassion. But deeper mindfulness practice reveals something different.

Weeks into one of my first long retreats, the teachers announced that Oxfam was asking people to make a donation and fast for a day in support of those in the world who don't have enough to eat. I'd been practicing mindfulness meditation on this silent retreat for many weeks. On hearing the announcement and reading the Oxfam literature the teachers posted, I felt deeply touched. Throughout the fast day I reflected that the hunger I was feeling only scratched the surface of what those in areas of famine must be experiencing. And, unlike their hunger, my fast was voluntary; I knew it could end whenever I chose. My heart burst open, and the next day, swept up with compassion, I wanted to just keep going with my fast. With no intentional metta practice, metta had arisen in a powerful way. I was advised against a longer fast in the context of such a long, intensive retreat, but the impact of that day stayed with me. I understood that it was awareness itself that had opened my heart, not a special practice.

Many teachers point out that a mind that is awake and aware, grounded in mindfulness, is naturally loving and kind. Joseph Goldstein in his book *Mindfulness: A Practical Guide to Awakening* says that as "our minds become more open and less defensive, we begin to experience metta as a basic quality of awareness." As the Buddha teaches, if we remove ill-will, what's left isn't a neutral state, but a loving one.

Metta cannot come to fruition without mindfulness, just as mindfulness lacking metta is dry and chilly. While our mind's tendency to categorize seeks clear distinctions, these two qualities and practices intermingle in a way that makes them essentially inseparable.

→ *practice*

MINDFUL METTA

As you practice metta meditation, begin to integrate elements of mindfulness. When you begin your practice, connect with the sensations in the body and the breath. Notice your mood and emotional state. Be aware of sounds in your environment and internally.

As you engage each element of the practice, note the sense of ease or resistance that comes with the different categories. See how your mind reacts to the thought of loved ones versus difficult people. Recognize the nature of the mind to cling to the pleasant and reject the unpleasant.

In this way you begin to integrate mindfulness and its insights with your metta practice.

eight

THE PURE-HEARTED ONE
Hindrances and Abodes

One of the first Buddhist meditation practices I learned is called "noting." In this practice, whenever you notice your thoughts have pulled you away from your breath, you make a silent mental note before returning to the breath. This note can be as general as "thinking, thinking," or as specific as "Aunt Martha" (assuming you were thinking about her). The version of this I found most illuminating involved noting whether a thought was one of desire or aversion. The reason I found it illuminating is that when I started to do this practice, I discovered that virtually every one of my thoughts was either one of desire or aversion.

Now I know this can be debated, and that strictly speaking certain loving thoughts or thoughts of generosity aren't desires in the sense that the Buddha was referring to. But these (in my case) few authentic instances of altruism are barely worth mentioning when put up against the steady stream of wanting and not wanting; of dreaming and judging; of irritation and nostalgia; of anxiety and regret. When faced with this deluge, it can be difficult to take seriously the Buddhist idea that one could be free from desire and aversion. Is that really possible? Is that a reasonable goal? And—wait a second—if it's a goal, isn't it a desire?

Desire and aversion are the first of the five hindrances, the classical list of impediments to meditation. The next two (or strictly speaking, four) are sloth/torpor and restlessness/worry. If you're not lost in your thoughts of desire or aversion, you're just as likely to be falling asleep or struggling to sit still. Sleepiness is mental and physical, a dullness that pervades body and mind. Restlessness is also mental and physical, an almost claustrophobic anxiety.

When facing these all-consuming obstructions to calm and concentration, to clarity and insight, one can easily be overwhelmed by the fifth hindrance, doubt. You begin to question whether the whole thing is worthwhile, whether you even have the capacity to sit still, to stay awake, to quiet the mind, or indeed to derive any benefit from these seemingly fruitless efforts.

Learning to meditate, at least in the early stages, is largely about learning to live with and manage these mental and physical obstructions. The hindrances or some variation of them are the source of most of the questions I'm asked about meditation. And what people usually want to know is how to make one or the other of them go away. I'm compelled to answer that the wish for a hindrance to go away is another thought of aversion, so it will only take you deeper into your struggle. Somehow we have to make friends with the hindrances. We can't think of them as the enemy, as something getting in our way. This idea, naturally enough, leads us back around to metta and the rest of the brahmaviharas.

Bringing the attitudes of the brahmaviharas to bear on the hindrances is one of the ways we can address them without creating more aversion. Rather than fighting with them, we apply a loving mindfulness to them, a gentle acceptance and investigation.

Here we find ourselves again at the beginning of metta practice, giving love to ourselves, wishing ourselves well. It's so easy when experiencing one or more hindrances to think there is something wrong with us or that we are meditating wrong, that we need to perfect our technique. But if we take the attitude that we are just experiencing the challenges of being a human being, it's easier to see that treating the hindrances kindly makes more sense than attacking them.

Working with the hindrances, then, is tricky because of course we want to be rid of them. The Buddha himself says we should "abandon" them. The issue is, how do we approach this abandonment, how do we view the process? If we see our spiritual practice as some sort of self-improvement project, then we by definition think we are flawed. We get so involved in this project that we don't see the inherent self-judgment in that attitude. Certainly most of us want to be better people, but if that involves berating ourselves, how is that supposed to help?

So, one way of addressing the hindrances is to try to bring the qualities of love, compassion, joy, and equanimity to bear on the feelings themselves—on the desire, aversion, sleepiness, restlessness, or doubt. So, for instance, if I'm judging someone in my mind, and I see how agitated that makes me feel, I bring an attitude of compassion to that agitation, wishing myself well. Notice that I'm not criticizing myself for being judgmental; judging is normal human behavior, not something aberrant that needs correction. Rather, I'm saying to myself, "It's painful to judge people, and it's not worth it." This approach teaches us to let go of judgment not because it's wrong to judge, but because it hurts. It hurts me. Seeing my own pain in any behavior is the most effective way to inspire change.

I can also remember to be compassionate to the one I am judging. If they are acting unskillfully or unwisely, I understand that they are probably experiencing some dukkha of their own. Not only that, but they are creating unwholesome karma through their actions, a further reason to offer compassion.

Another way of applying the brahmaviharas to the hindrances is a practice known as "replacing." This is found in a sutta entitled, appropriately enough, *The Removal of Distracting Thoughts* (MN 20). Here we intentionally bring to mind something different from that which is distracting us. So, for instance, if there's a sense of lack triggering desire, we practice loving-kindness, which helps us feel more fulfilled, more complete. When there is sadness, we practice appreciative joy to uplift our spirits.

With four brahmaviharas and five hindrances, that makes for a whole lot of potential relationships. I wonder if I can make the connections a little simpler.

Let's just say that the hindrances are a bunch of unpleasant mind and body states: we want stuff, we don't want other stuff; we're tired or edgy; we're confused or frustrated.

Then, let's say that the brahmaviharas are a bunch of pleasant mind and body states: we love stuff, we care about stuff, we enjoy stuff, and we're not bothered by stuff.

As much as anything, applying the brahmaviharas to the hindrances—or "replacing"—is about trying to bring these more positive attitudes to our experiences. As we train in the meditative aspects of the brahmaviharas, we become both more familiar with them and more adept at arousing them. Then, in both our meditation and our daily lives, we more easily evoke these attitudes and these states when needed.

"Attitudes and states" are what I called in "May I Be Happy" (chapter 1) "seeing and experiencing." Sometimes we can just find a different way of viewing a situation—a different attitude—and that will shift how we feel. This can happen when instead of being angry at another driver, we remember to be compassionate for their situation. This shift in attitude, then, causes our state to shift as well. Now, instead of being agitated by a reckless driver, I feel care and concern for them, and my experience changes. Maybe they are late for work or on the way to the hospital. Barring that, just the fact that they are so stressed that they feel compelled to drive dangerously means that they are stuck in some kind of dukkha. This new state is one of calm and acceptance. It's much more pleasant than the aversion felt in judging another driver.

States are developed through meditation practice. When states of calm, openness, and happiness are present, we're not even bothered by the driver who cuts in front of us. We just apply the brakes and continue with our day.

I prefer this approach, which I'd call intuitive and organic, to the more formulaic ones sometimes offered. Blending the brahmaviharas with the hindrances is a natural thing to do. You don't actually have to be familiar with any of these teachings to do it. Many people figure this out just through their life experience. It is helpful, though, to have this framework to fall back on.

Whether through noting, replacing, investigating, or simply accepting, the hindrances must be addressed in our meditation and in our lives.

→ *practice*

HINDRANCES AND BRAHMAVIHARAS

Here are some suggestions for countering the hindrances with the brahmaviharas:

- **Sensual desire:** If you cultivate joy in your life, you'll feel less needy and driven by craving. Sympathetic joy suggests an appreciation of beauty and happiness around you that arouses gratitude, one of the most reliable ways of bringing joy.

  Equanimity helps you detach from desire, creating a sense of spaciousness and balance. With this more settled mind, you feel less prone to craving.

- **Anger/ill-will:** First work with loving-kindness to connect with a more positive state. Then focus on compassion for yourself as well as the object of your anger. Compassion for yourself will show you how you are creating pain inside with your anger. Compassion for the other reminds you that their unskillful behavior is driven by their own suffering.

- **Sloth and torpor:** Here again, sympathetic joy can be used to bring energy. Bringing to mind the joy of others can evoke positive mind states.

- **Restlessness and worry:** Cultivate loving-kindness to help you settle back. The agitation of restlessness is soothed by thoughts of kindness.

- **Doubt:** Cultivate compassion to remind yourself that practice is not just for you. If you are questioning the value of your practice, you might find motivation and inspiration in the wish for beings to be free from suffering.

nine

ABIDING IN EQUANIMITY
Concentration and
the Brahmaviharas

My discussion of *The Shorter Discourse in Gosinga* in chapter 2, "Like Milk and Water," stopped before a dramatic shift took place in the sutta. Up until then, the conversation between the Buddha and Anuruddha had been solely about how the monks were getting along, how they were living together. For no apparent reason, to the casual reader, the next thing the Buddha asks Anuruddha is if they have "attained any superhuman state . . . a comfortable abiding."

How do we go from talking about how we keep our campsite clean to attaining superhuman states?

It turns out that the sutta is actually following a very common, traditional form that the Buddha used in his teaching: sila, samadhi, panna—or morality, meditation, and wisdom. The principle is that moral and ethical behavior lay the foundation for concentrated meditation, and concentrated meditation lays the foundation for the arising of wisdom. The part of the sutta I discussed before was primarily about sila, loving-kindness in action. Once the Buddha establishes that the three monks have been living with skillful sila, in harmonious relations, he goes on to inquire how their concentration is developing.

And, surprise, surprise, it's going great!

In fact, Anuruddha goes on to say that they've developed the deep concentration states called *jhana* that often appear in the suttas. This section of the discourse is probably a cut-and-paste job, since much of what Anuruddha says appears in the same words in other suttas. This is one of the characteristics of the suttas, that when they get to a place where they're going to discuss something that's commonly taken up, it will appear in a formulaic pattern.

It's worth asking, though, why would sila lead to samadhi? A simple answer comes from Ajahn Pasanno who told me, "The intrinsic effect of wholesome mental states is that they are settled and peaceful." In other words, if your behavior is kind and non-harming, if you aren't creating conflicts or doing things to feel guilty about, you tend to be less stressed, less agitated. There just aren't that many things to disturb your mind, so you can more easily get concentrated.

Loving-kindness actually involves both sila and samadhi. Sila is the behavior and samadhi is the meditation practice. While the Buddha didn't give extensive loving-kindness practice instruction in the Pali Canon, the *Visuddhimagga* develops a systematic form. This consists of repeating phrases of loving-kindness first to yourself, then to a teacher or benefactor, to loved ones, a neutral person, and a difficult person. Then we radiate love to all beings. Most teachers suggest doing this while still feeling the breath and visualizing those we are sending love to. Finally, there is a focus on the felt sense of loving-kindness in the body. This combination of elements can bring the mind into a state of balance and calm that's highly conducive to concentration.

While paying attention to the breath in mindfulness practice doesn't give us much to hang on to—the breath being pretty subtle and having no dramatic attraction—metta practice requires us to more or less fill the spectrum of awareness with words, breath, images, and sensations. To hold all these elements simultaneously in our awareness makes it difficult for anything else to slip in and distract us. This accounts for the concentrating effect of metta.

This concentration is enhanced and deepened when paired with the joy of metta. When thinking of dear ones, a feeling of happiness naturally arises. This uplifting feeling inspires our hearts and minds to sink deeply into the experience of concentration and joy, creating a kind of feedback loop that takes us even more deeply into calm and concentration. Finally love, peace, joy, and clarity blend together into a seamless experience.

One simple gateway into the joy of concentration is to smile. Even statues of the Buddha often depict a subtle turning up of the corners of the mouth. Smiling triggers pleasant feelings, and those feelings help focus the mind. But this idea wasn't one that I came to naturally.

I have a memory of walking down the street when I was about eight and passing some teenage girls who looked at me and said, "Smile!" I gave them my best eight-year-old sneer and walked on. This early tendency to dismiss smiling as a trivial act stayed with me as I grew up and even well into my thirties. So you can imagine my skepticism when I encountered Thich Nhat Hanh's meditation called "Present Moment, Wonderful Moment," which includes the instruction to smile.

My teacher at the time had studied with Thây (as he's known to his followers) and brought back a practice called *gathas*, or verses. Thây created gathas for all kinds of daily activities as a way to help maintain mindfulness. Then there was this gatha, specially designed to aid in following the breath:

In, out
Deep, slow
Calm, ease
Smile, release
Present moment, Wonderful moment

Repeating the words with the breath is a way to calm the thoughts, as well as evoke a positive mind state. My teacher said that when we got to "smile, release," we should bring a slight smile to our face and leave it there. "Don't force it," he said. "Just turn up the corners of your mouth." Although I wasn't any less cynical at that point than I'd been at eight, I was a little more willing to try things people suggested.

I hate to admit it, but those teenage girls were right. I should have smiled.

The gatha practice wasn't something I did in order to feel happy, at least not consciously. It was a concentration practice, something meant to aid the mind in staying on the breath. I found it very helpful in this regard. It was repetitive like a mantra or a breath-counting practice, but it wasn't so tedious. It had a brightness to it that felt uplifting. While it starts with simple phrases that point toward mindfulness, it moves toward loving-kindness with the "smile" and "wonderful moment." So it's blending those practices, but with a third goal: the development of concentration.

The gatha on mindfulness of breathing became my main practice for about five years. Over that time my practice became much more joyful and the smile took me into new realms of concentration. Here I discovered what the Buddha was talking about in his teaching on the seven awakening factors. These include the factor of joy, *piti* (sometimes called rapture).

When I first came to practice, the idea that joy would be part of the path didn't resonate for me. I thought of meditation as serious, a slog through the mire of my mental states; a struggle with sleepiness and knee pain; at best, a heroic struggle to conquer my imperfections. Joy didn't seem to have anything to do with it.

But as I smiled, day after day, sit after sit, my heart opened and my mind settled, then expanded.

Metta is embedded in Thây's gathas. It evokes the same qualities of joy and tranquility. Its structured form gives us something steady and consistent to hold to, bringing calm and focus to the mind. Even as we smile, we are doing what the Buddha suggests: radiating kindness, in this case, to ourselves.

I think there is a tendency for the meditator when trying to develop concentration to think it comes about through making a great effort, that you need to focus more strongly to quiet the mind. This attitude often leads to more struggle, a battle with the mind. Smiling brings another attitude, one of acceptance and even humor. After watching our own mind for a while, smiling at what we see makes at least as much sense as frowning. Truly, the behavior of our minds is absurd. The judgments and opinions; the expectations and fantasies; and the simple repetitive nature of our thoughts just don't make much sense. When we realize that joy is a foundation element of concentration, then turning meditation into a battle stops being our strategy. Our attitude lightens up, and instead of judging our mind, we start laughing at it.

What a relief.

→ *practice*

CONCENTRATED METTA

There are at least two ways to orient ourselves toward developing concentration in our metta practice:

1. Fill the mind with a combination of breath awareness, body awareness at the heart, metta phrases, and images of the objects of metta. Holding all these elements in awareness simultaneously tends to absorb the mind. We have to maintain a delicate balance that keeps our attention clear and sharp. This combination of elements also creates a spacious or open effect in the mind.

2. In contrast to the open effect, the second approach is to make the attention very narrowly focused on the metta phrases. We zero in on these words, blocking out all distractions. If we notice the mind wandering, we immediately bring it back to the phrases. This creates a sense of being held in a safe, cocoon-like mental state.

ten

RADIATING KINDNESS
The Practice of Metta

It may have surprised you in reading this book that I haven't yet given specific guidance on the form and mechanics of loving-kindness meditation. I've been more interested in metta as an attitude or perspective, as well as understanding the subtler nuances and implications of the brahmaviharas, what it means to live with love, care, appreciation, and balance. There are, in fact, many techniques for loving-kindness meditation, just as there are for mindfulness and concentration, and while I favor certain ones, I think it's wise for each practitioner to experiment to see how they work and which is best for them.

Rather than any particular technique, what I think is most important in the development of our practice is the time and commitment we put into it. It's our devotion and strength of intention that sustains practice, and sustained practice is what brings the most transformative results.

Nonetheless, we all need somewhere to begin, some form to hang on to at first, so I'll pass on some suggestions later in this chapter.

It isn't surprising that a practice designed to deepen our heart connection is one that brings out creativity in meditation teachers. While some teachers adhere closely to the *Visuddhimagga*'s guidance, many forge entirely new approaches to teaching metta.

One of my favorite metta teachers was Ayya Khema, the German Buddhist nun. Her approach was a "radiating" practice that used imagery. On retreat, she would guide metta each evening, often using a fresh image each time. Sometimes it was a golden light emanating from the heart. Other times a lake filled with metta where you invited more and more people until all beings were swimming together in loving-kindness. This style of practice works well for someone who is more visually oriented.

The standard practice involves using phrases directed toward various individuals and groups. Repeating these phrases can work like a mantra, stilling and focusing the mind. I've used this practice a great deal as well.

I know some teachers will claim that the meditation form they teach is the best one. I'm skeptical when I hear these claims. My sense is that these teachers had success with a particular form, and they assume that it must be the best, since it worked for them. Naturally enough, teachers teach what works for them, but I think we should be careful in assuming that because something works for one person it will work for everyone. I try to offer a variety of approaches to practice in my own teaching, but even with that effort, I know I lean toward certain forms that work for me.

The Buddha himself didn't give much actual instruction for how to practice metta meditation, at least not that was recorded in the suttas. As we'll see in the next chapter, he said that we should wish, "In gladness and in safety, may all beings be at ease." From this instruction we extract three of the classic metta phrases: "May you be happy [gladness]; may you be peaceful [at ease], and may you be safe." Later in the *Metta Sutta* he tells us to "radiate kindness over the entire world." In other suttas he talks about spreading each of the brahmaviharas in all directions. Since this didn't give us much to go on, the *Visuddhimagga* developed a more detailed and structured system that has been adopted by many teachers.

When we look carefully at this system, it's apparent that Western teachers and practitioners have adapted different aspects to their own needs and preferences. What's most obvious, as I talked about in chapter 1, is that the early Buddhist teachings assume we all love ourselves. That's presented as a simple fact. While the *Visuddhimagga* describes many challenges and blocks to metta—such as impatience, resentment, lust, and irritation— it never suggests that arousing love for oneself will be a challenge. This fact alone is cause for finding different approaches to metta than the *Visuddhimagga* offers.

Many teachers start by teaching a forgiveness practice as prelude to metta. This is done as a kind of cleaning the slate before diving in. As I described in the meditation instructions earlier, forgiveness is practiced for yourself, for the ways you've harmed yourself; for others who have harmed you; and asking forgiveness from those you have hurt.

After working through this process, we start to practice metta. Here are some reflections on the purpose and challenge of each of the elements of the *Visuddhimagga* method of metta.

Elements of Metta Meditation

DISCOVERING METTA: The *Visuddhimagga* begins its instruction on loving-kindness by saying one needs to "review the danger in hate and the advantage in patience," because we "cannot abandon unseen dangers and attain unknown advantages." In other words, we need to know what we're trying to let go of and what we are trying to develop. We need to see how hatred harms us and how patience helps us. This is a quality of right view, understanding the workings of karma and the Noble Truths.

On a more basic level, we need to understand the purpose of meditation practice. People often enter into spiritual practice out of some vague longing or fantasy about what it's about—I know that's how I started. But after a while, when no magic happens, we begin to question the actual purpose of sitting around paying attention to our breath. This is actually a good question to ask and can help focus and deepen our practice. With metta practice the answer to this question is what I've been trying to write about in this book.

Along with some understanding of the purpose of practice, entering the practice involves connecting with the actual experience of metta. We need to know what loving-kindness feels like in the body and in the emotions. Given that the *Visuddhimagga* assumes that we feel love for ourselves, it opens by saying to focus on ourselves. Since, as I've said, many of us in the West don't have such a simple relationship with ourselves, I think it can be more helpful to start with someone else. This isn't a matter, for me, of dogma or "proper technique," but simply a practical answer to the challenge of beginning to feel the quality of metta.

BELOVED/BENEFACTOR: The initial stage of practice is particularly important because we are trying to establish the felt sense of metta. While we may not be able to keep the same level of loving feeling for others as we progress through the practice, this at least clarifies the aim at the start.

The "benefactor" refers to someone who has been of great help to you in your life, often a teacher or mentor. Many meditation teachers have modified this person to more generally call them a "beloved person." The idea of the benefactor probably goes back to a more devotional, guru-oriented spiritual practice wherein just the thought of the teacher would inspire great faith and love. As Western Buddhism, especially Theravada and the insight tradition, have largely forgone this approach, it seems simpler to just focus on a beloved person. Everyone might not feel that they've had a benefactor.

The main point of starting with a beloved or benefactor is to arouse a pure, unadulterated feeling of non-sensual love in the heart. This allows us to, first of all, identify what love feels like in the body, in the mind, and in the heart. And it brings a pleasant mood to the mind, which makes it easier to concentrate and relax. We could say that we are setting the stage for the practice with this first recipient of our metta.

When we think of a benefactor, we often feel a sense of gratitude, and gratitude has been shown to be one of the most effective ways to bring about a positive mind state.

What is *not* encouraged is that one use one's spouse or lover for this stage, because of the risk of falling into lust, which, because it is one of the five hindrances, will block the arising of metta as well as concentration. Besides, given the complexity of such relationships, there is also the risk of some negative thought or feeling slipping in.

I'll add that it's also suggested that we use only living people for this stage of practice. This is, again, related to concentration, as the arising of grief might block the calming of the mind. However, I would just take this as a suggestion, and if you are drawn to reflecting on lost loved ones, just be careful that your practice doesn't veer into sorrow and grieving. Try to focus on a positive memory rather than the sense of loss.

Some teachers go so far as to suggest using a pet or animal to arouse initial loving-kindness. Remembering cat videos you've seen on YouTube may not seem very "Buddhist," but if it works as a trigger for metta, why not? For myself, the strongest trigger I've ever felt was my infant daughter. During her first few years of life whenever I thought of her while on retreat, the metta veritably exploded. Interestingly, while she is still just as precious to me today, there simply isn't the same visceral effect now that she's grown—perhaps it's a failure of my own imagination.

SELF: Once we've worked with the beloved/benefactor and developed the feeling of loving-kindness, we turn toward ourselves. The logic of this suggestion is simple: we can't truly love others if we don't love ourselves. In that case, we might be trying to make ourselves feel better by loving other people or trying to get them to love us. One who loves themself doesn't depend on others for a sense of well-being or self-esteem.

As I talked about in chapter 1, many people struggle with the idea of loving themselves. Because they know they are imperfect or because they know all their own failings, they feel unlovable. Or, because of painful emotions, when left to just contemplate themselves, they don't feel loving. In other words, if you are depressed, it's hard to love yourself—or anyone else.

How do you work with these feelings?

One suggestion—and this applies to anyone we find it difficult to love—is that "We don't have to *like* them (or ourselves), we just have to love them."

What does this mean?

Liking ourselves means we evaluate our assets and deficiencies and decide whether we deserve love, whether we've earned it. Love, on the other hand—at least metta—is unconditional, not dependent upon being earned or on our worthiness. It is something we deserve *because we are human* or maybe more generically, *because we are alive,* or maybe even more generically, *because we exist.*

To take this perspective, it can help to pull back from our self-identification and see ourselves as just a human being subject to the challenges and struggles of life, someone who has succeeded and failed, suffered and felt joy, with all the longings and disappointments of this worldly realm, this realm of samsara. And, dare I say that if you are someone who is trying to practice loving-kindness, you are *already* someone with powerfully positive motivation to live skillfully and surely deserving of love. If there is anyone not deserving of love, it certainly isn't the person who is consciously and intentionally trying to develop the quality of metta.

Giving metta to ourselves is easier and more natural when the mind quiets down. When we can sit with a simple awareness of the body, alive and breathing, we step out of self-consciousness into the visceral sense of being. This body, this breath, this fragile life, calls for care, compassion, and love. In this primal experience, we feel the preciousness of existence that naturally opens the heart.

As with any meditation practice, it takes time to settle the mind and heart. It's important to put in the time to ride out any resistance or agitation. Time is the great healer in meditation, impatience the enemy.

DEAR ONES: This third category is perhaps the easiest and most enjoyable to practice. Here we send metta to everyone we care for. We can start with those who are closest to us, our family and dear friends, letting each person float through our attention, whether as an image or a name or a felt sense. If you are regularly doing this practice, you might organize these people. I go through my family by thinking of my brothers first (my parents are dead), from the oldest to the youngest (there are four), then their children and wives and any grandchildren. Then I see whatever friends might come to mind. When I'm on retreat and want to extend this practice, I sometimes take my mind down the block where I live where I have warm feelings toward many of my neighbors and their children. Anything that helps your attention to stay focused is useful. While it's not necessary to have an organizational system, it can certainly help.

This part of practice can be so pleasant that we don't want to move on. I think we have to be careful here, though, that we aren't just using the practice to feel good. While those feelings can support our concentration, if we come to rely on pleasant experiences in meditation we will inevitably face some disappointment because feelings are impermanent and must surely pass.

NEUTRAL PERSON: This is perhaps the most difficult part of the practice to explain, even though most people in the world are neutral to us. We are simply looking for someone to focus on toward whom we don't have any positive or negative feelings. This almost certainly means we don't know them well, which is fine. Currently I use the guard in the parking lot at my bank. I see him regularly and can easily visualize him, and I don't have a relationship with him.

The first purpose of working with the neutral person is to see that even people we don't care about want the same thing we do: to be happy. When I see this clearly, I begin to have a different view of living beings; we are all after the same thing, whether we know it or not and whether we are going about it in a wise way or not. In order for metta to be realized on its most essential level, we must learn to care for all beings, and since most of them are neutral for us, this is a good place to start.

Another purpose in working with the neutral person is to begin to move the neutral people into the dear camp. After one retreat where I used a local video-store clerk as my neutral person for a month straight, I walked into the store and my heart exploded with joy and love in seeing him—and I didn't even know his name. Great faith in this practice arose in that moment. I saw how this training really works; it's not just about being nice or thinking good thoughts. It can actually transform my heart and mind.

DIFFICULT PERSON: Arriving at the difficult person brings us to a "simile of the saw" moment—well, perhaps not that radical, but at least we must face our ill-will. Before we can abandon or uproot these tendencies, we have to see them clearly. With this practice we confront how deeply embedded anger or resentment is in us. Having developed an understanding behind the philosophy of metta, we now have a chance to put that philosophy into practice. If everyone deserves love and if anger only hurts the angry person, then we should be able to send loving-kindness to a person with whom we've had conflicts or toward whom we have ill-will. However, "should" is rarely an effective motivator and certainly doesn't change how we feel.

As with the neutral person, the idea is to train the mind. Keep practicing, even in a mechanical way, and changes will gradually happen. Keep breathing with the unpleasant feeling and trying to arouse some kind of positive thought or feeling.

The *Visuddhimagga* suggests that with the difficult person, our first goal should just be to move them to the neutral camp. If we can defuse the explosive anger and turn down the heat of resentment, we can potentially soften our feelings to the point that they lose power.

This part of the practice also gives us insight into the limits of our capacity to love and shows us where we get stuck. Are my difficult people family? Friends? Ex-partners? A boss or colleague? Or maybe your biggest resentment is toward a political figure.

What surprised me when I began to do some of this work was how many of the people who had hurt me, I had also hurt, and that they were also my dearest—my parents and siblings. I couldn't see them as my "difficult" people, but there were clearly complicated feelings involved.

The broader point is that ill-will takes many forms and attaches to many different people and things. While there may be truly hateful feelings toward certain people, we likely also carry subtler forms of irritation, impatience, and annoyance toward many others. Working with this category can be hugely revealing, and will probably give us a lifetime's opportunities for practice.

RADIATING: Once we've passed through all these categories, we begin a less personal phase of the practice. In theory, you would have abandoned ill-will at this point, having practiced metta toward the difficult person. In my experience, that isn't necessarily true, but nonetheless, it doesn't prevent you from moving into the radiating practice.

In the radiating practice, you are working with a sense of space, first nearby and gradually expanding. You can continue to use phrases, like "May all those in this room be happy," as you spread loving-kindness outward, but I find that at this point the words actually get in the way of my felt experience. You can try different approaches for yourself.

The idea with radiating is that you are essentially carpeting the world—and even the universe—with loving-kindness. Various images or feelings can be used for this. One, suggested by Ayya Khema, is to imagine a golden light radiating from a lotus in your heart. The light spreads outward farther and farther, touching all beings its reaches. If imagery helps you, this, or anything similar, is a good way to work with this aspect of practice.

Another way to connect with radiating is more a felt sense of expansion. As the mind gets concentrated in metta meditation, the boundaries of the body seem to soften, and when you start radiating, you can imagine that those boundaries disappear. Now there's a sense of consciousness and heart-love moving naturally outward from your physical location. This is what the Buddha means by a "boundless heart." As self-consciousness falls away, the sense of separation also dissolves, and we can easily and naturally have a sense of expansion. In this practice we inject love into that expansion.

In practical terms, the way I practice radiating is by first filling the room I'm in, then the building, neighborhood or campus, city, and then just pushing outward across land and sea until I'm surrounding and permeating the earth with loving-kindness. Then you can radiate out into space until the ends of the universe.

Of late, because of my concern for our planet and its inhabitants, I've stopped after spreading metta over the earth. This has been an emotional decision because I'm just so aware of the suffering and harm being done on and to the earth that I almost feel as if focusing on the rest of the universe almost trivializes these problems. And, in fact, that is true. Compared to the expanse of this universe, the problems on this tiny planet are trivial. But my heart weeps for this fragile blue orb drifting through space. Perhaps as I get older I'm becoming too sentimental.

Once we've reached the limits of radiating, it's helpful to hang out there for a couple of minutes, just feeling that vastness of heart and consciousness. Then, gradually imagine you are coming back, back into the room you are in, into your body, your heart, your breath. At that point, acknowledge that the powerful sense of limitless loving-kindness you've just experienced comes from your own heart and is always available.

CATEGORIES: You can do the process of expansion in the spatial/geographic way I've just described, but you can also add categories of beings to make it more explicit.

I often do contrasting categories, such as "those who are sick and those who are well; those who are at war and those at peace." But you can do anything you like. When we focus on people who are suffering, we are essentially taking our loving-kindness practice into the realm of compassion, the next of the brahmaviharas. Technically, you aren't supposed to do that, mix the practices, but in reality, I find it difficult to keep them apart. I'd say it depends on your intention in doing the practice, whether you are trying to develop precise, delineated states or whether you are more generally interested in opening your heart and feeling connected.

This previous description of the aspects of loving-kindness practice shows how you can do the whole range of practice in one sitting. However, many teachers offer retreats that work through the different types of people much more slowly. Days might be spent just focusing on self, on loved ones, on neutral, or on difficult people. The latter method is an even more systematic form.

→ *practice*

LOVING-KINDNESS

Settle into your posture, relaxing with some deep breaths and letting your attention come into your body. You should be sitting upright, balanced, and aligned, without tension in the body.

Bring your attention to the center of your chest, what's called the heart center, near the solar plexus. You might have a visceral or emotional feeling there. Try to have a sense of opening your heart, of being vulnerable and receptive.

Next think of someone who is very dear to you, someone who it's easy to love without distraction. Bring their image to mind or just the thought of them. Then begin to repeat phrases of loving-kindness for them. Use three or four phrases. You can use the following suggestions or adapt or make up your own.

"May you be happy, may you be peaceful, may you be safe."

Keep the phrases going in concert with the breath, one breath for each phrase. Smooth, slow, and steady.

Remember how much you love this person, and connect with that feeling in your body. Have a sense of the love you have for this beloved person pervading your body.

Continue to repeat the phrases.

Now you are combining mindful breathing with an image, with phrases, and with the feeling of love in the body. Try to balance your awareness of all these experiences in your mind.

Next bring loving-kindness to yourself.

"May I be happy, may I be peaceful, may I be safe."

Continue this for several minutes.

Then bring to mind all your dear ones, friends and family. Continue with the phrases for each person.

"May you be happy, may you be peaceful, may you be safe."

Continue this for several minutes.

Next think of a neutral person.

"May you be happy, may you be peaceful, may you be safe."

Continue this for several minutes. Be aware of when the attention wanders, and bring it back to the phrases and the breath.

Then think of a difficult person, either someone with whom you have struggled or a public person who troubles you.

"May you be happy, may you be peaceful, may you be safe."

Continue this for several minutes, noticing any resistance or emotional reaction.

Next begin to "radiate" loving-kindness, filling the room you are in, the building, then outward to the neighborhood, the city, and beyond. Finally send loving-kindness to all beings on earth and to the earth itself.

Finally, radiate kindness outward into space until you have a sense of filling the entire universe with loving-kindness. Rest in that vast space of love for as long as feels helpful.

Bring the attention back into the room, into the body, into the heart, and into the breath.

Rest in the calm and openness of loving-kindness.

Note: This practice can be done at different speeds. You probably need a minimum of ten minutes to go through it all, but at a slow pace it can easily last forty-five minutes or longer.

eleven

THIS IS WHAT
SHOULD BE DONE
The *Metta Sutta*

It's remarkable that the *Metta Sutta*, a short teaching of just a couple hundred words, covers almost everything I've written so far in this book. This most beloved Buddhist sutta covers sila, samadhi, and panna; non–ill-will, mindfulness, and the hindrances; and even the four stages of awakening. According to Bhikkhu Bodhi, it is viewed as a protective and blessing teaching. Nonetheless, it is also quite explicitly an instructional text. While originally delivered to and for monastics, with just slight interpretation, laypeople can draw a lifetime's lessons from the challenging teachings of the *Metta Sutta* (Sn 1.8).

We know it's an instructional text because the sutta begins by telling us, "This is what should be done." Kind of like saying, "Sit up and pay attention, folks."

The translation I first encountered gave the next line as "by one who is skilled in goodness, and who knows the path of peace." Right away we might question what this means. If you already know the path, why do you need all these instructions? I've heard and read various responses to this, including the idea that the sutta was delivered to monks who had already attained "stream entry," the first stage of enlightenment, and, in contrast, that it really means "who *wishes* to know the path of peace." Since my main concern isn't technical, for the purposes of "unenlightened worldlings" like myself, I'll take it to mean, "If you know what's good for you, this is what you should do." I mean, is there any reason you *shouldn't* follow this sutta if you don't "know the path of peace"? The fact is, absorbing the profound teachings of the Buddha and the Pali Canon already takes a fair degree of spiritual evolution, so even if you aren't already in the stream, you're probably at least sitting on the banks watching it flow by, maybe thinking about dipping a toe in.

While much of the Pali Canon is now available to Western Buddhists, I'd been practicing for twelve years before I encountered this, my first sutta, in 1992. Even though I was living in Northern California by then, I was once again sitting in Joshua Tree at Dhamma Dena, the same retreat center where I took my first retreat, this time with Ruth Denison, the founder of the center. She distributed photocopied sheets of the sutta so we could chant together. I was thrilled to have this direct teaching, and delighted in the harmonious chanting we did together. I took that sheet home and decided to look for the first thing the sutta said you should do and take that on as a practice.

After "the path of peace," the next lines are "Let them be able and upright, straightforward and gentle in speech." I found able and upright a bit vague, though now I understand that it refers to living with sila. Nonetheless, I decided I would try to be "straightforward and gentle in speech." It turned out to be a bit more of a challenge than I'd imagined—in fact, I'm still trying to learn that one twenty-five years later.

The sutta goes on to list more behaviors and attitudes one should strive for:

Humble and not conceited,
Contented and easily satisfied,
Unburdened with duties and frugal in their ways.
Peaceful and calm and wise and skillful,
Not proud or demanding in nature.
Let them not do the slightest thing
That the wise would later reprove.

Now over a quarter of the way into the sutta, what do you notice? Nothing has been mentioned about loving-kindness. We're being told what kind of a person we should be: humble, moral, wise. Like the opening of *The Shorter Discourse in Gosinga*, this is addressing practical concerns and personal qualities, such as not being demanding and being frugal.

Encouraging humility and discouraging pride are ways of guiding us away from ego inflation and self-centeredness. Weakening these qualities is one of the principal goals of Buddhist teachings and practices, as the Buddha teaches that trying to gratify the ego is one of the primary causes of suffering. Being contented and undemanding then points to another of these causes, seeking after sense pleasure, viewing accumulation, stimulation, and acquisition as ultimate goals for attaining happiness. Though this section speaks specifically to monastic ideals, they're easily appreciated and adopted by laypeople.

Clearly the Buddha is encouraging a life of simplicity, and here is where the layperson's challenges diverge from the monastic who can, perhaps, more easily or at least justifiably, shed duties. The fact is, no matter how few or many our duties, their burdensome quality is largely a function of the mind. Do we take on duties as burdens or do we hold them lightly? If we stay present from one action to the next, from one duty to another, they don't have to be overwhelming. I've come to see this instruction as relating as much to attitude as to behavior: keeping calm and peaceful in the midst of life's complexities.

Only now does the Buddha begin to give instruction on loving-kindness.

"Wishing: In gladness and in safety, may all beings be at ease." This is pretty much it, the heart of the matter. As we saw in chapter 10, we should wish for all beings to be happy ("in gladness"), peaceful ("at ease"), and safe (safe from their own minds and safe from other people's behavior). What the Buddha is suggesting is not complicated. It's summed up in a single line, that we should wish for others well-being.

The following half dozen lines just find ways of saying, "I'm talking about everyone. Don't leave anybody out."

> Whatever living beings there may be;
> Whether they are weak or strong, omitting none,
> The great or the mighty, medium, short or small,
> The seen and the unseen,
> Those living near and far away,
> Those born and to-be-born—

If you have any thoughts of exclusivity, of one person or group deserving loving-kindness more than another, banish those from your mind. This includes nonhuman beings as well. The commentaries on the sutta suggest that these instructions are helpful because they give us specific people to focus on. These same commentaries (found in Bhikkhu Bodhi's translation of the Suttanipata) give complex and technical explanations for these categories. For me, those aren't really necessary. I get it. Love everybody.

Whenever I read or chant this sutta, I'm also struck by the variation in tone, from the more poetic lines ("May all beings be at ease") to the ones that land with a thud. "Medium, short, or small" makes it sounds like you're choosing T-shirt sizes.

The section is wrapped up by repeating the admonition, "May all beings be at ease."

Now we enter the section of the sutta that addresses the theme of *The Simile of the Saw*: non–ill-will.

Let none deceive another,
Or despise any being in any state.
Let none through anger or ill-will
Wish harm upon another.

Now he is describing how we *shouldn't be* and what we *shouldn't do*. In my years of doing this practice, I've come to see this as my greatest challenge. It's not difficult for me to love people I care about. Sure, there are times of conflict, but when I really think about them, my heart opens. And I find somewhat the same effect when reflecting on the human race or all beings in general. It's the difficult people, the politicians I disagree with, the ones I rant about when reading the news; it's the editors who rejected my books and the record company executives who turned down my demo tapes; it's the health insurance company that rejects my claim, and, yes, the driver who cuts me off on the freeway. These are the challenges to my metta practice.

Now we can also see that the sutta is indirectly giving instruction on following the five precepts. Here we're told not to lie (fourth precept) and not to wish harm (first precept). The earlier instruction on frugality references the second precept (not to steal), and the general admonition to not do anything the wise would frown upon infers following all the precepts.

The following phrase is one of the most revered in the Pali Canon:

Even as a mother protects with her life
Her child, her only child,
So with a boundless heart
Should one cherish all living beings;

The image of a mother's love, just as Ajahn Jumnien had told my wife and me when we met him with our infant daughter, epitomizes the idea of metta. It also gives us another explanation of how to do loving-kindness practice: cherish all beings; hold them dear.

But I think we need to look a little further at this image to get its full effect. The idea of "mother love" is kind of romantic, soft and gentle. But here the Buddha is talking about a mother actually sacrificing her own life when her child's life is threatened. So, once again, we actually have an image that implies violence—not as explicitly as having your limbs sawed off, but nonetheless a fierce, determined, and heroic love, not just sweetness and light. Is the Buddha saying we should be willing to sacrifice our own lives for the lives of every other being? His own reflection on his behavior in a past life can shed some light.

A Jataka tale depicts the Buddha in a previous existence coming upon a sick tiger mother who was starving and unable to feed her cubs. Out of compassion he threw himself off a cliff to give the tiger mother food. As a Buddha looking back, he said that, while this obviously reflected great compassion, in the end it was not a skillful act. Killing yourself to save the life of another is still killing.

So, I think we can infer that the Buddha isn't so much saying we should be willing to die for other beings as that our love should be as strong as a mother's. This brings us back to the question of what metta really is. While a mother's love is usually affectionate, its underlying drive is to care for her children, to protect them. Caring for someone, acting in their interest, is a greater expression of love than the emotion we feel for them.

The next lines give more instruction:

Radiating kindness over the entire world:
Spreading upwards to the skies,
And downwards to the depths;
Outwards and unbounded,
Freed from hatred and ill-will.

We're back in poetic and inspiring language. Not only should our loving-kindness be for everyone, it should be everywhere. In fact, these lines aren't even referring to people, or beings of any kind. They refer to the sky and the earth. I'll explore this idea further in chapter 13 on nature.

Notice, too, that this passage starts by recommending kindness and ends by telling us to be free from hate. How, one might ask, could you radiate kindness without being free from hate? I don't think you could, but I just think the Buddha wants to emphasize over and over how insidious hate is, how it can slip in even when we think we are being loving. We need to be vigilant.

"The depths" probably also refers to the hell realms, which are described in early Buddhist literature. Similar to Christian visions of hell, in these realms beings are subject to unspeakable pain and horrors. The only difference is that, while Christian hell is eternal, banishment to the Buddhist hell realms is temporary—although in this case "temporary" apparently means thousands of years.

For contemporary Westerners, these hell realms are usually viewed as metaphorical, the hell of mental and physical suffering. Mark Epstein's *Thoughts without a Thinker* does a good job of showing how the realms, which include animal, human, hungry ghost, jealous god, and god realms, match up with different states of happiness and pain in human existence.

This section ends with more instruction, and a description of the practice:

> Whether standing or walking, seated or lying down
> Free from drowsiness,
> One should sustain this recollection.
> This is said to be the sublime abiding.

Here we have a prosaic description of the four postures in which the Buddha says we can practice mindfulness. Then we are reminded about the hindrance of sloth and torpor. In fact the sutta has already given instruction on three other hindrances: desire is addressed when we're told we should be "easily satisfied" and "frugal in our ways"; aversion is repeatedly addressed in the plea to avoid ill-will and hatred; restlessness is discouraged in the words "peaceful" as well as "ease." The antidote to doubt is studying the teachings and practicing, so just by engaging the sutta, we weaken that hindrance.

The phrase "sustain this recollection" makes explicit the connection between loving-kindness and mindfulness. "Recollection" is another translation of *sati*, the word for mindfulness. If we are trying to practice loving-kindness, as I've talked about earlier, we have to be mindful; otherwise, when the mind wanders, we don't know it. Mindfulness protects metta, keeps it on track. Of course, this also requires concentration, which is the essence of sustained attention.

The final line from this section points to the name the Buddha gave for the four qualities of the heart he encouraged. "A sublime abiding" is essentially a brahmavihara. *Brahma* refers specifically to a god realm, but we know from many suttas that the different realms can easily be understood as mind states; *vihara* is a living place, usually one reserved for monastics, and so "divine abodes" is the usual translation, but "sublime abiding" says the same thing.

The last four lines of the sutta take such a radical turn that I think they deserve their own chapter. So, let me review how I see the structure of the sutta so far:

- A lengthy opening encouraging wise, moral behavior and a peaceful, undemanding attitude.
- One line of instruction for wishing that people be happy, peaceful, and safe, followed by an extensive description of who these different people are.
- Another section focusing on non–ill-will as opposed to love.
- The comparison of metta to a mother's protection and the instruction to spread that care everywhere.
- The encouragement to practice this in all postures and to keep the practice going all the time—in the same way the *Satipatthana Sutta* tells us to practice mindfulness in all circumstances.

twelve

NOT BORN AGAIN
INTO THIS WORLD
Awakening

This is the chapter I've been dreading. Enlightenment? Awakening? What do I know about those things? And besides, what's that got to do with "living kindness"? I'd skip the whole topic if I didn't feel it would be a betrayal of the project. After all, the closing verse of the *Metta Sutta* tells us that fulfilling this teaching will bring a breakthrough in consciousness. But before I explain all that, let me tell you a little about my relationship to the issue.

One of the first things that attracted me to Buddhism was the idea that I would become "enlightened." I had my own ideas of what this meant, and they didn't have much to do with what the Buddha actually taught, since, at that time, I didn't know anything about what the Buddha actually taught. These ideas were somewhat vague, since they included otherworldly experiences that I had never had and could only imagine. But I did believe that if I were enlightened I'd never be depressed again—this was a priority for me. And I also assumed that all my meditations would be very peaceful, even blissful. I thought I might have some superhuman powers, though I wasn't really concerned about this. It just seemed kind of cool to be able to walk through walls or be in two places at once. Then I included things like never having to worry about money. And, absurdly enough, way in the back of my mind was an assumption that my musical career would take off and I'd be a rock star. I know how crazy that sounds, and it wasn't that I had this conscious thought, but I basically thought enlightenment meant the end of all my problems and the satisfaction of all my wishes. Of course, that's not anything like what the Buddha said about enlightenment.

I kept up this delusional thinking until I got sober, at which time the whole idea of enlightenment lost its allure. I realized I had more immediate, worldly problems to deal with and set about working on them. My new priorities became employment, education, and healthy relationships. The "spiritual awakening" that the Twelve Steps talked about seemed much more practical and simple. It was mostly about sila, service, and kindness.

I progressed on all fronts, obtaining a BA and MFA, then a solid job in the tech world. Soon, I was married with a child on the way. My practice had also ripened to the point that I was becoming a meditation teacher as well. Now a more grounded understanding of the Buddha's teachings combined with a deeper experience of concentration got me thinking maybe I *could* have this breakthrough. I learned that the Pali Canon described four stages of enlightenment. The initial one, called stream entry, was supposed to put you firmly on the path to the rest of the stages, to make inevitable that in this life or some future life you would attain full enlightenment.

Of course, this then brought in the question of rebirth, another sticky issue, to say the least. For the moment, I preferred not to think too deeply on that one, but focused more on my meditation. I began to look for markers or indicators of where I was on the path, and a couple of my teachers were very encouraging.

Sadly, whatever was supposed to happen didn't happen, and as I entered my sixties and went through a couple more episodes of depression, I went back to a simpler view of practice as a healing and sustaining activity. Just as I was settling into some comfort and acceptance about my shortcomings, two of my monastic teachers, Ajahn Amaro and Ajahn Pasanno, came out with a book called *The Island*, which was a compilation of quotes from the Pali Canon on enlightenment. Their stated purpose on publishing the book was to encourage people to strive for stream entry. They said that they felt people had lost interest and inspiration in pursuing this vital breakthrough.

This threw me into another state of doubt and confusion. Was I giving up too easily? Was I lacking in real commitment? Or, on the other hand, did I lack some personal quality that would allow me to have this breakthrough? And then came the biggest doubt of all: Was enlightenment real?

Sure, the Theravada tradition has a pretty explicit description of the four stages of awakening, but what actually occurs or how they really play out is less than clear. And while this particular tradition has its own version of what happens, so too do other Buddhist traditions, each claiming to be the authentic one. Jack Kornfield's essay "Enlightenments" does a pretty good job of muddying the waters among the major Buddhist traditions, while tossing in a couple of other religions as well. His premise is that there are many different manifestations of enlightenment and that none is any better than any other. They're all equally valid. This seems a little like youth sports teams that don't keep score and give all the little soccer players participation trophies. No winners, no losers. Safe, but unsatisfying. It's easy when looking at all this to throw up your hands and say, as do the Korean Zen masters, "Don't know." And clearly I don't.

But this book isn't supposed to be about enlightenment or transcendent states anyway, is it? So, let me come back to my original theme by asking: What is the relationship between "enlightenment" and living kindness? In fact, is there one? There have been several supposedly enlightened Buddhist masters whose behavior was clearly harmful, who were alcoholic or took sexual advantage of students—and sometimes both. If an enlightened person can be a drunk and an abuser of women, what is the value of enlightenment? And, in fact, can someone who behaves this way actually claim to be awakened? It brings to mind words attributed to Suzuki Roshi: "Strictly speaking, there are no enlightened people, there is only enlightened activity." That sounds closer to what I'm getting at.

Let's look at the last four lines of the sutta to see if we can gain any understanding about what "enlightened living" might look like.

> By not holding to fixed views,
> The pure-hearted one, having clarity of vision,
> Being freed from all sense desires,
> Is not born again into this world.

According to Bhikkhu Bodhi, these four lines actually encapsulate three of the four stages of enlightenment. He says stream entry includes "not adopting wrong views, impeccable conduct, and insight into the four noble truths." He skips the stage of "once returner," but says that ending sense desires leads to the third stage "non-returner," that is, one who won't be reborn but will become fully enlightened in this lifetime. Finally, the last line describes the *arahant*, the fully enlightened one who is not subject to rebirth.

That's all well and good, but if we haven't had those four "path moments," or even one, how can we understand these lines?

Start with fixed views. If you can hold your opinions more lightly, you will certainly get along with people better. The stubborn need to be right only alienates others and limits our capacity to learn and grow. If we already know everything, we're closed to new information and new points of view. That Korean Zen "don't know" idea really comes in handy here.

When we think about the conflicts and limitations in our lives, many are there because we have unexamined opinions that we live by. These beliefs—about self, about others, about anything from politics to sports to morality to metaphysics—are often deeply conditioned, deeply embedded in our psyche. We adopt and maintain these beliefs because they make us feel safe, in control.

My own ideas about who I was and what my capabilities were held me back from any emotional or even professional growth. As a teenager I fell into depression and became disenchanted with school. Depression makes it hard to do anything, to care about anything, or to show up for challenging responsibilities. At the same time, music was becoming my refuge, the one place where I felt happy and free. Out of these contrasting feelings and experiences, I developed a belief about myself: I needed to be a musician; nothing else would make me happy. And because I was beginning to fail in school and didn't have any other obvious talents, I believed that I wasn't capable of being anything but a musician. In this way, my beliefs about myself narrowed my choices and defined the unfolding of my life for the next twenty years. "Holding to fixed views" about myself crushed my life. It was only when I got sober and finally saw through the delusion of those beliefs that my life began to change. I found out that my limiting beliefs were in fact completely wrong.

Ajahn Pasanno points out how holding a fixed view is one way that we cling to an identity; who I am is largely defined by what I believe. This clinging is one of the major sources of suffering, so that, as he says, "even if your view is correct, holding it with a sense of self is still suffering!" So it's not that having a view or opinion is a problem—that's somewhat inevitable. Rather, what's critical to our happiness is how we hold the view—in a fixed way or in an openhanded way.

In the time of the Buddha spiritual seekers debated a set of metaphysical questions and defined themselves by their answers to these questions, things like "is the universe eternal?" or "do enlightened beings exist after death?" The Buddha said it wasn't helpful to hold opinions on these things. We know that philosophers through the ages have chosen different topics to debate, usually questions for which they could never give a definitive answer. The Buddha sees this sort of speculation as a distraction from what is really important: ending suffering. In fact, his point is that holding on to these ideas actually sustains suffering, gets in the way of ending it.

In the next line, what is this "pure heart" the Buddha is talking about? In the most basic terms it's the openness of love and compassion. There's a quality of innocence and simplicity in the fundamental wish for everyone to be happy, to be safe and at ease. While some might call such a stance naive, when we really tune in to our experience we see that the self-seeking approach to life is painful and leaves us empty and lonely. Keeping a pure heart—or at least "purish"—brings a lot more peace than a hateful, lustful, or greedy heart.

Clarity of vision? I think we can safely say that meditation and Dharma study give us a clear view of things, and that view makes life go much more smoothly. This is, after all, what vipassana meditation means—to see clearly. While we might come to meditation with grandiose ideas about its benefits, to see things clearly is an elemental aspect of living wisely—and kindly.

Okay, "freed from *all* sense desire"? Maybe not, but how about not letting sense desires run your life? How about seeing how cycles of craving cause suffering? I think we can agree on that.

If we let pleasure rule us, we get caught on a constant wheel of craving, chasing stimulation from one moment to the next. The Buddhist practice, whether mindfulness or loving-kindness, trains us to sit with whatever is arising—pleasant, unpleasant, or neutral. We learn to be less affected by these variations, more able to maintain balance in the buffeting winds of change. This doesn't mean we'll stop wanting tasty food or a satisfying sexual relationship, but it means, hopefully, that those things won't dominate our thinking to the point of dukkha. For those of us who haven't attained complete awakening, navigating this tightrope of seeking comfort without grasping is one of the great challenges of our practice and our life.

Finally, the relevance of not being born again can be applied to creating ego, to not inflating yourself and your importance in the world. As some Buddhist teachers say, we can think of rebirth as what happens every time we "create a self" in a moment. Every time I grasp on to a view or opinion, every time I think about me, every time I take a stance or project my ego, I am creating a self. *Samsara* literally means "wandering on," says

Ajahn Pasanno, and he goes on, "when we stop the 'wandering on' of self, of mind, we are not born again."

I'm not going to pretend that this is a full representation of these closing lines, but if we are not at the point of having all these breakthroughs, what are we supposed to do with these teachings? Throw them out? Say they don't apply to us, so we'll just ignore them? That doesn't seem sensible or in accord with the Dharma.

I think we need to hold both the literal translations of scholars like Bhikkhu Bodhi as well as the practical applications of teachers like Ajahns Amaro and Pasanno. It's not "either-or." There's some transformative insight that can occur on this path. But that's not by any means the only benefit of practice. Awakening is a process, and from the first step to the last, benefits and transformations are evident. If this path is going to make any sense for us, we must live it day by day, while never putting limits on our potential for awakening.

thirteen

OVER THE ENTIRE WORLD
Metta for the Earth

Recently some friends came to visit from Ireland and the UK, and I took them to see various sites in the Bay Area. First we drove to Sausalito, where we could view the houseboats on the Bay, Angel Island, and the skyline of San Francisco. Then we took a walk out onto the spectacular Golden Gate Bridge from which we could see Alcatraz and the Farallon Islands. Next I said I would take them to Muir Woods.

"Woods?" they asked. "Why go there?"

I told them they'd have to trust me. It would be worth it. Once there, they understood. Some of these remarkable trees have been alive for a thousand years and stand 250 feet tall. While other sites in Northern California may be more iconic, these ancient redwoods draw some of the largest crowds of tourists. But I don't think it's their age or their height that ultimately impresses people. Rather it's their presence. As you walk deep into this forest, something happens to you, a feeling of peace and serenity emanating from the trees drapes you. People's voices become softer or go silent. They walk slowly, as if in a temple or cathedral. And, indeed, there's no better comparison than to the experience of entering the medieval cathedrals of Europe. The power of these trees' presence is undeniable. It's a call to something primal in our own nature, our connection to the earth.

The relationship between trees and humans—or anything that breathes—is intimate and essential. We breathe out, they breathe in; they breathe out, we breathe in. Simple as that. Absolute interdependence.

I don't know if the Buddha understood this in a scientific way, but he must have intuitively. His first instruction in the *Satipatthana Sutta* is to "go to the forest or to the root of a tree" and practice mindful breathing. Leaving the urban areas and going into the forest was a tradition for seekers in ancient India and is emulated by the contemporary Thai Forest Tradition. While I'm not aware of anything explicit in the Buddhist teachings pointing to the meaning of this relationship, the implicit message is that the forest holds spiritual significance.

Perhaps this is the subtext of the origin story of the *Metta Sutta*. While helping his monks overcome their fear of "tree spirits," he was also telling them to love nature, to be kind to the trees and the earth.

A PhD thesis could probably be written about the Buddha's relationship to trees: his mother hanging onto a tree branch to birth him; the experience as a child under the rose apple tree that pointed his way to awakening; his enlightenment beneath the bodhi tree; and his death between two sala trees. But the more important point is the whole relationship to nature that's expressed in the suttas. The Buddha often used metaphors and similes drawn from nature: the handful of leaves, the spoonful of salt in the Ganges, and the stone mountain worn away by a cloth. The four elements—earth, air, fire, and water—are a repeated theme, and he often draws on images of oceans, forests, and wild animals. One of the most enduring images, captured in many statues, is of the Buddha touching the earth to affirm his awakening against Mara's challenge. I don't believe any of the Buddha's teachings were given by accident. I believe he was trying to remind us, over and over, to recognize our connection with the earth, to respect it, and to show it the love it deserved as our "Mother."

In *The Shorter Discourse in Gosinga*, the monk who cleans up throws the leftovers "where there is no greenery or drops it into water where this is no life." Here we see a sensitivity to the environment that would fit nicely with our modern sensibility. The Buddha taught his monks to be very aware of any harm they might do to the earth.

What's apparent in the suttas is that even the Buddha couldn't imagine the level of harm modern humans would inflict on the earth. In *The Simile of the Saw* several images suggest that nature is too great, too vast to be seriously affected by human activity. When a man tries to dig up the earth, he finds it futile because you can't "make this great earth to be without earth." In another sutta (MN 62) he says that the earth isn't disturbed by people throwing "urine, pus, and blood" on it. And yet today we know that, while the earth can't be "without earth," it can certainly be damaged by fracking, overgrazing, strip-mining, clear-cutting, and many other human activities. The brutal mountaintop-removal mining is a particularly violent kind of decapitation that seems cruel and even hateful toward the earth. As desertification spreads, we see that the land, from which we derive all our sustenance, can be damaged to the point of uselessness.

When a man tries to draw pictures on empty space, nothing happens, because space is "formless and invisible." But we now know that the air can be polluted to the point that breathing becomes unhealthy and dangerous, an issue exacerbated by clear-cutting the oxygen-producing equatorial rain forests that are considered "the lungs of the planet."

The image of setting the Ganges on fire to dry it out reminds me of the time the Cuyahoga River in Ohio caught fire because of the incredible level of toxic chemicals that had been dumped in it. Worse still is what is happening to the ocean, the vast ocean, as it becomes warmed and acidified to the point that life is dying out.

No, I don't think the Buddha could have imagined what we've done to the earth. On the other hand, he would have perfectly well understood how we got here, how ignorance and greed, hubris and the belief in our own supremacy over nature may be driving us to the point of killing ourselves by making our planet unlivable.

The Buddha would have understood the greed that drove people to exploit resources with no regard for the environmental consequences; he would have been familiar with the hatred that makes people think of nature as an enemy to be conquered; and he would have seen clearly the delusion that allows people to think there will be no serious consequences for their treatment of the earth, air, and water on this planet. Yet, even as he understood these impulses, and perhaps even had compassion for those under their thrall, there's no doubt he would have seen these behaviors as the most egregious abuse of the gifts afforded by nature.

I find it quite telling that Bhikkhu Bodhi, who spent decades consumed with scholarly work in a monastery in Sri Lanka, has come down from the lofty perch of Dharma study to found Buddhist Global Relief. He shows us that no matter how deep our Dharma practice and study, we should never divorce ourselves from the reality all around us, the reality of human suffering, and how the Four Noble Truths are manifesting in the world.

When we read the Greed, Hatred, and Delusion Report, it's easy to get caught up in all kinds of controversies—political, economic, and social. But it seems to me that one issue must take precedence over all the others: the environment. Without clean air and water, without productive soil and fisheries, human life won't survive on this planet. All other issues pale in comparison. Without the requisites for life, humanity—and perhaps all life—will die out, the most egregious break possible of the first precept not to kill any living beings. Is this scenario impossible? I don't know. But it's clear that we are on a path that could lead to mass starvation, wars over drinkable water, climate catastrophe, and a planet that verges on unlivable.

When I heard someone's idea that the solution to an unlivable earth is to move to another planet, I wanted to cry. After despoiling one paradise, we'll just move on to another disposable world. If that's the lesson humans take away from our environmental disaster, we really don't deserve to survive as a species.

If, as Buddhists, we place protection of life as our highest value, then we must respond to this threat. This is where the practice of metta and all the brahmaviharas becomes urgent, stepping out of the realm of spirit into reality.

Standing beneath the majesty of Muir's redwoods, one can't help but think about how they've lived since William the Conqueror invaded England and Genghis Khan swept across Asia; they were around when Gutenberg invented the printing press and Da Vinci painted the *Mona Lisa*. They were here when enslaved people were first brought to North America and when they were emancipated. Many French Louis and English Georges have passed; Washington and Napoleon have come and gone; world wars and genocides have not touched them. But can they survive the change of climate that descends upon us? The fragile balance of temperature and moisture from coastal fog creates a unique environment in which they've thrived. All this is changing, though. While this little grove of trees on the western edge of the continent holds no particular importance in the planetary scheme, they are just one more of the trillion natural manifestations that this earth has brought forth. Will our blindness and arrogance destroy them all?

Ultimately it is only our love that can save them.

With these reflections on the environment in mind, I've added some elements to my metta practice. I often still follow the traditional format of sending love to myself, to my dear ones, to a neutral person, and to a difficult person, then "radiating" loving-kindness to all beings. Nowadays, though, I find my love turning toward the earth as well as individuals.

Though the *Metta Sutta* tells us, "Even as a mother protects with her life, her child, her only child," now I think it's time for the children to take care of the mother—our only Mother Earth. After all, at this time in history, the human race has done so much damage to its mother that she may no longer be able to take care of us. What a tragic turnabout.

The Buddha says we should "radiate kindness over the entire world, spreading upwards to the skies and downwards to the depths, outward and unbounded free from hatred and ill-will." If we take this instruction literally, it can be used as a practice for the earth. The skies are sick with the carbon and toxins we have fed into them; the earth punctured, injected, poisoned; the seas suffused with plastic and floating gyres of junk. In my metta meditation, all of these wounds have been healed: I see clear skies, a radiant blue deeper than any living person has ever seen as every building is topped with solar panels and, through renewable technologies, we have ceased spewing filth into the air; I see the soil fresh and pure, regenerated through sustainable farming practices; I see the frackers packing up and going home; and finally I see the oceans bright and clean as all the ships from all the navies of the world sweep the oceans clean and vacuum its floor of the detritus of plastic waste. This is my vision.

To open our hearts in this way takes us beyond self and even beyond humans to the source of our life: this fragile and wounded planet. Here is a way to do this practice.

→ *practice*
METTA FOR THE EARTH

Breathing into my heart, I feel my connection to the air and atmosphere all around me.

Breathing out of my heart, I radiate love to the air and atmosphere, seeing it protected and healed.

The sky is bright and blue; the air precious and pure.

Breathing into my heart, I feel my connection to the earth beneath me.

Breathing out of my heart, I radiate love down into the earth, seeing it protected and healed.

The earth is vibrant, green and fragrant with life.

Breathing into my heart, I feel my connection to the sea from which all life arises.

Breathing out of my heart, I radiate love to the sea, seeing it protected and healed.

The sea is clear blue, bright and shining.

I hold the entire planet and all living beings in my heart with love, care, and compassion.

May this planet be safe; may it be healed; may it be free from suffering.

Afterword

My goals in writing this book were twofold. First, I wanted to expand people's understanding of the meaning of loving-kindness, how it applies to our lives internally and externally. Second, I wanted to inspire people to explore the suttas of the Pali Canon. These can seem intimidating and confusing, but I hoped to show that it wasn't necessary to read hundreds of suttas or be a Buddhist scholar to benefit from their study.

Those ideas aren't where I started, though.

My initial impulse was to write a book about modern consuming behaviors as addictions that are destroying the environment, as in "America is addicted to oil," and then tie that to the Dharma. While this seemed like a good premise, when it came to the writing, the ideas simply weren't there. Instead I found myself drawn into this exploration of metta.

Thus, what became the last chapter of this book was actually the first one I worked on.

Finally, if you think that I wrote a book about living kindness because I'm such a loving and sweet person, think again. Or talk to my wife and daughter. I probably fall more into the category of "teaching what I need to learn." As I've said before, I find the ideals the Buddha puts forth both inspiring and intimidating. After some forty years of practice, I can still feel like a beginner. But, for some reason I've been given a platform to write and teach, so I do my best to offer something of value.

I will tell you this, though: I delighted in writing this book. I hope you benefited from reading it.

Love, love, love . . .

Acknowledgments

My work on this book has been directly and significantly aided by two people:

Ajahn Pasanno read an early draft and gave vital guidance around technical and sutta aspects. His support of the project helped my confidence in its value immensely. Several of the quotations attributed to him come from his notes on the manuscript or my conversations with him. Wes Nisker acted as a structural editor and guide to improving the readability of the text. His suggestions for revision were key in helping me keep the book vital and personal. I am deeply grateful to these generous friends and teachers.

Without Bhikkhu Bodhi's work translating the Pali texts, this book wouldn't exist. He also kindly answered several of my technical questions. Most references to statements of his are based on his audio course "A Systematic Study of the Majjhima Nikaya."

Sharon Salzberg's work is the other foundation of the book.

Venerable Analayo continues to challenge and inspire me with his work on the Pali Canon.

Thanks to Amanda McPherson for proofreading the first edition, and to Walt Opie for the author photo.

Mike Campbell did a beautiful cover and interior design for an earlier version of the book.

Thanks to Peter Schumacher at Shambhala Publications for being a great partner in bringing this book to a wider readership. And thanks to everyone at Shambhala who has worked on and shepherded this project. The design, editing, and marketing teams have done creative, careful, and valuable work through trying times. I appreciate all the effort you have made to enhance the book.

Glossary

Pali Terms

arahant—A "worthy one"' one who has eliminated all defilements and attained full liberation in this very life.

bhikkhu—Monk. The feminine is *bhikkhuni*, although the Buddhist scholar Venerable Analayo says the original meaning of bhikkhu wasn't assigned gender.

brahmavihara—Divine abodes, a metaphorical name for metta, karuna, mudita, and upekkha. These are seen as the purest and highest spiritual emotions, thus "divine."

deva—A god or angel.

dukkha—Suffering or unsatisfactoriness. Dukkha is the subject of the Buddha's key teaching, the Four Noble Truths.

jhana—Meditative absorption; deeply calm states of concentration. In the suttas there are either four or eight of these states.

karuna—Compassion.

metta—Loving-kindness.

mudita—Sympathetic joy, appreciative joy.

panna—Wisdom or insight, the outgrowth of developing sila and samadhi.

piti—Rapture or bliss; the main quality of the first jhana.

samadhi—Concentration or meditation; mind training.

samsara—The cycle of birth, aging, death, and rebirth characterized by a fruitless wandering in search of satisfaction.

sangha—Traditionally, the community of enlightened monks; more generally today, the Buddhist community.

sati—Mindfulness.

satipatthana—Foundation of mindfulness. This is the name of the sutta that gives the Buddha's most thorough exposition of mindfulness practice.

sila—Morality or ethics. This is the foundation for spiritual practice, living a life of integrity.

sutta—Teaching or discourse.

upekkha—Equanimity.

vipassana—To see clearly; insight. This is a term used to describe the practice the Buddha taught in the *Satipatthana Sutta*. Today it is usually referred to as insight meditation. Secular mindfulness uses this as the basis for meditation practice. While clearly coming out of the Theravada Buddhist tradition, at times vipassana is offered as something disconnected to any tradition, almost a tradition unto itself.

Sanskrit Terms

There are a couple of words that have both Sanskrit and Pali spellings for which I chose the Sanskrit, simply because it is better known.

Dharma—The Truth (capital *T*); natural law. This also refers to the teachings of the Buddha, which are considered Truth. The Pali is *Dhamma*.

Karma—Literally "action," though the term usually refers to the law of karma, which says, "all actions have results and all results have causes." Actions take three forms: thoughts, words, and deeds. Each of these is said to have results. The Buddha redefined karma as "intention," that is, the motivation behind our actions, which he said was the real cause determining the results of an action. The Pali is *kamma*.

References and Resources

Books

Amaravati Buddhist Monastery, *Chanting Book*, vol. 1. Hertfordshire, UK: Amaravati Publications, 2015

Analayo, Bhikkhu. *Compassion and Emptiness in Early Buddhist Meditation*. Cambridge, UK: Windhorse Publications, 2015.

———. *Satipatthana: The Direct Path to Realization*. Cambridge, UK: Windhorse Publications, 2003.

Batchelor, Stephen. *After Buddhism: Rethinking the Dharma for a Secular Age*. New Haven, CT: Yale University Press, 2015.

Bodhi, Bhikkhu. "A Challenge to Buddhists." *Lion's Roar*, September 1, 2007. https://www.lionsroar.com/a-challenge-to-buddhists/.

———. *The Connected Discourses of the Buddha: A Translation of the Samyutta Nikaya*. Somerville, MA: Wisdom Publications, 2000.

———. *The Numerical Discourses of the Buddha: A Translation of the Anguttara Nikaya*. Somerville, MA: Wisdom Publications, 2012.

———. *The Suttanipata: An Ancient Collection of the Buddha's Discourses Together with Its Commentaries, Translated from the Pali*. Somerville, MA: Wisdom Publications, 2017.

Epstein, Mark. *Thoughts without a Thinker: Psychotherapy from a Buddhist Perspective*. New York: Basic Books, 1995.

Fronsdal, Gil, trans. *The Dhammapada: A New Translation of the Buddhist Classic, with Annotations*. Boston and London: Shambhala Publications, 2005.

Goldstein, Joseph, *Mindfulness: A Practical Guide to Awakening*. Boulder, CO: Sounds True, 2013.

Kornfield, Jack. "Enlightenments." In *Bringing Home the Dharma*. Boston, MA: Shambhala Publications, 2011.

Nanamoli, Bhikkhu, trans. *The Path of Purification: Visuddhimagga*. Onalaska, WA: BPS Pariyatti Editions, 1999.

Nanamoli, Bhikkhu, trans., and Bhikkhu Bodhi, ed. *The Middle Length Discourses of the Buddha: A New Translation of the Majjhima Nikaya*. Somerville, MA: Wisdom Publications, 1995.

Nhat Hanh, Thich. *Call Me by My True Names: The Collected Poems of Thich Nhat Hanh*. Berkeley, CA: Parallax Press, 1999.

Pasanno Bhikkhu. *Abundant, Exalted, Immeasurable*. Redwood Valley, CA: Abhayagiri Buddhist Monastery, 2016.

Salzberg, Sharon. *Lovingkindness: The Revolutionary Art of Happiness*. Boston: Shambhala Publications, 1995.

Web

Access to Insight, a sprawling source of translations and commentary on the Pali Canon: https://accesstoinsight.org/.

Bhikkhu Bodhi's audio course "A Systematic Study of the Majjhima Nikaya": http://bodhimonastery.org/a-systematic-study-of-the-majjhima-nikaya.html.

Also by Kevin Griffin

Buddhism & the Twelve Steps Daily Reflections
Buddhism & The Twelve Steps Workbook
A Burning Desire: Dharma God and the Path of Recovery
Laughing Buddha (music CD)
One Breath at a Time: Buddhism and the Twelve Steps
(also available as an audiobook)
Recovering Joy: A Mindful Life after Addiction